Wirecraft

Wirecraft

Kramer, Jack

John Highstone

Drawings by Michael Valdez

*Photographs by Matthew Barr
and Clark Photo Graphics Studio, San Francisco*

Houghton Mifflin Company   Boston 1978

Library of Congress Cataloging in Publication Data

——— (date)
  Wirecraft.
  1. Wire craft.   I. Title.
TT214.3.K7   745.56   78-15538
  ISBN 0-395-26297-6

Printed in the United States of America

A 10 9 8 7 6 5 4 3 2 1

Book design by Martha Lehtola, Designworks, Inc.

Contents

Wirecraft

Introduction

For most of us, the word *wire* brings to mind something as prosaic and practical as the coat hangers we bring home from the dry cleaners. Yet in recent years, artists and sculptors have taken wire out of the closet and used it as the medium for creating articles of beauty and imagination. Now, following their lead, craftspeople are finding that wire is an amazingly versatile, inexpensive material with which to make articles that are useful as well as decorative. Wire is inexpensive — you can make a coffee table for as little as $3 or a magazine rack for $5 — and is easily obtainable from a hardware store. You can even use those coat hangers. A soldering gun or iron and a few pairs of pliers are just about all the tools you need.

The projects in this book range from very easy to fairly complicated, from a simple candle snuffer to a complex candelabra. In size, they range from a decorative frog to a tall plant stand. For each of the twenty-four projects, you will find exact patterns and step-by-step drawings, plus, of course, instructions in the techniques of working with wire. Eventually, we expect, you will want to make most of the objects you see here — for your home, to give as gifts, or to sell at a fair or bazaar; but if you have never worked with wire before, start with one of the simple projects. Even while learning, you'll find working with wire a fascinating craft, one that provides hours of pleasure in the work and years of pleasure from the finished projects.

You can buy wire in coils, on spools, and in handy packets at hardware stores and surplus outlets. The large coils are 12- and 14g, packets are 18g, and spool wire runs 24g to 30g.

1 A World of Wire

Wire is a versatile material that comes in many forms and sizes. Look around your house for a moment: there are wire coat hangers in your closet, a wire whisk in your kitchen, wire spokes on the bike tires in your garage, and wire strings on the guitar. But these are only wire objects you can see — what about all the wire used within your phone, television, radio, and stereo, and the wire in the foundations and walls of your home? Indeed, there are more than 150,000 practical uses for steel wire alone. And that number doesn't include the new uses which artists and crafts people are finding for this material.

Thicknesses and Types of Wire

To make decorative and useful household items from wire, you first must know something about the material itself. Wire is a flexible material capable of assuming many forms; it has shape and dimension and strength. In working with wire you need some basic tools and knowledge to make a finished product correctly. In the following pages we will cover all these areas, but, for now, let us look closely at wire.

Wire comes in several diameters; the diameter is the *gauge* of wire. The 11- to 17-gauge wires are the most practical for wirecraft. (Wire coat hangers are about 12 gauge, to give you an idea of the thickness of wire within the 11- to 17-gauge range.) The almost threadlike 30-gauge wire is good for some joining methods used in wire projects. In our projects we use several gauges of galvanized wire. For general information, wire is sized as follows:

Wire Gauge	Diameter in Inches
12	0.1055
14	0.1080
16	0.0625
18	0.0475
20	0.0348
22	0.0286
26	0.0180

The most common wire, and the one you will probably use for many projects, is galvanized wire, which is inexpensive and can be bought at most hardware stores. You can also buy steel, copper, aluminum, and brass wire, or you can salvage wire from such items as coat hangers and lamp shades. (When I was a paper boy I made toy sculptures from the wire used to bale the papers.) Here is a rundown of the various kinds of wire.

Galvanized Wire.   This inexpensive wire can be soldered, glued, shaped, and painted without difficulty. Galvanized wire comes in many gauges, from 30g (very fine) to 12g. The 12-, 14-, and 16g wires are very useful for household items. Baling wire is a kind of galvanized wire.

Brass and Copper Wire.   Sold in both hard and soft finishes, these durable and strong wires are excellent for decorative crafts and are easy to shape and work with. Both kinds of wire are somewhat more expensive than galvanized wire.

Picture Wire.   This is twisted wire, generally of brass or copper, and excellent for braiding and lacing (joining) wires.

Silver and Gold Wire.   Used almost exclusively for jewelry making, these are expensive but have a handsome look.

This is 14g wire as it comes off a coil.

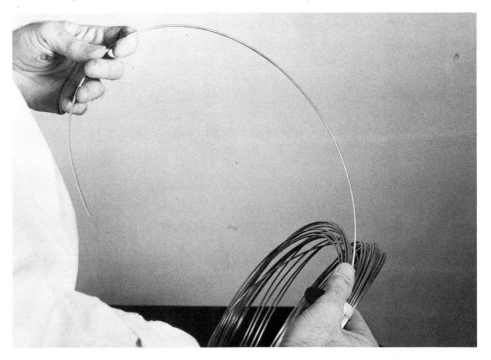

12

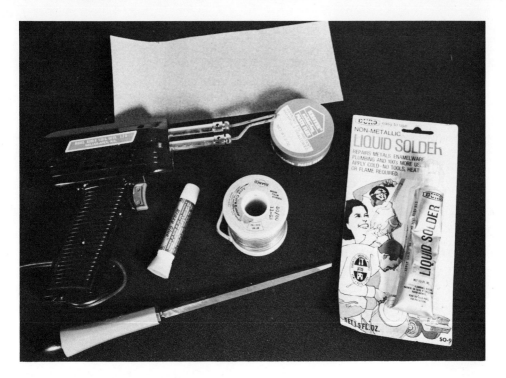

Some tools and equipment for soldering are: soldering gun (or iron), and fluxes. The file at front is to nick the wire so the solder will hold at joints. You can also use sandpaper.

Stovepipe Wire.   A black, very flexible wire, this is excellent for braiding unions (braiding is discussed in Chapter 3). It comes in several gauges; use 22- or 24g for your wire projects.

Plastic-coated Electric Wire.   This very flexible though not esthetically pleasing wire is useful for making playthings and odds and ends.

Aluminum Wire.   This wire is very flexible (even thick aluminum wire can be formed with ease), tough, lightweight, readily available, and can be easily polished to a high luster. It is excellent for household items. Soldering aluminum is somewhat more difficult than soldering other wires because it quickly develops a thick oxide layer. Use special fluxes and solders at a higher temperature for aluminum. And most importantly, be sure to scrape and file wires where joints will be.

Hardware Cloth.   This is screen wire that comes in several mesh grinds. It is inexpensive and available at hardware stores. Cut it with tin snips.

Florist Wire. Florist wire is thin but pliable and can be used for tying joints.

Salvage Wire. Salvage wire is old wire from objects like bedspring coils, electric apparatus, and coat hangers. It can be used, but aside from coat hanger wire, which is easy to work (see Chapter 5), most preformed manufactured wire is difficult to bend and form. If you find some old coiled wires, you might try to use them, but do not be too disappointed if they do not work as easily as you had expected. Still, for those who have access to used wire, experimenting with it is worth a try.

Wire Properties

Wire possesses four major properties: hardness, tensile strength, malleability, and toughness. *Hardness* is an indication of how easily wire will scratch or can be dented. *Tensile strength* refers to how much longitudinal stress wire can take without snapping (for example, copper has ten times the strength of tin). *Malleability* is related to hardness and is the ability of wire to be beaten flat without splitting or cracking. If you are forging wire, a wire's malleability is most important. Gold wire is the most malleable. *Toughness* indicates whether wire will twist and bend readily. One measure of toughness is elasticity, the ability of wire to recover its normal form after being compressed, stretched, or twisted. Toughness also refers to how easily wire snaps or fractures under pressure.

Buying Wire

Wire is sold in coils. Hardware stores carry small coils, while larger coils are available from wholesalers (look in the Yellow Pages for wire wholesalers). The small coils are not too expensive and work well for most projects. A small coil contains 25 or 50 running feet; larger coils may have 200 feet or more. This is a lot of wire, but it is cheaper to buy in quantity.

Bailing wire is sometimes sold in bulk, by the pound. This wire is 12- to 16g in size, with varying degrees of hardness — the softest is the best for household items. You have to buy at least 100 pounds of baling wire, so you may have more wire than you ever wanted.

Very fine wire is coiled on spools, like thread, and can be used in many projects that do not require sturdiness. (Save the spools because they make great sculpture forms.) Jewelry suppliers carry fine wires.

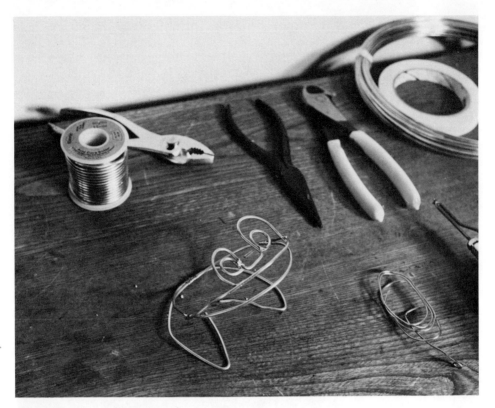

Pliers are an essential part of wire-craft working.

Cutting sheet metal.

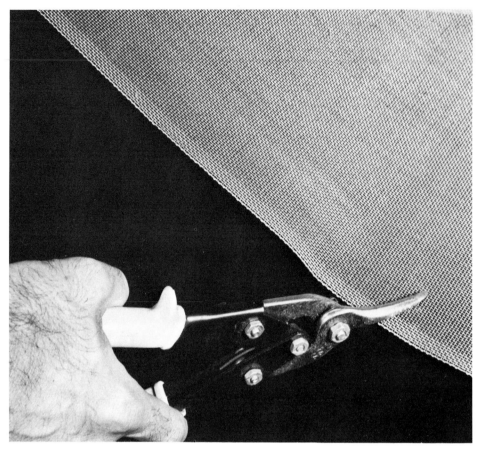

Here hardware cloth is cut with snips.

Sheet Metal

Sheet metal in various thicknesses is sold at hardware stores and heating shops. You can buy it by the piece, and for some of our projects (decorative leaves, for example) you will need some very small pieces and tin snips to cut the metal.

There is nothing difficult about cutting sheet metal; the hard part is handling it because the sharp edges can cut. So wear gloves when working with this material. Draw the pattern with grease pencil on the sheet, cut to the pattern, and be careful of the sharp edges. Work from the outside of the pattern to the inside, manipulating the small square of metal with one hand while cutting with the other hand.

When you have cut the patterns, bend and shape the metal into the forms you want. If the metal is too tough for hand work, use pliers until you can form the material properly.

Tools

Working with wire involves few tools and equipment. First you need some *pliers*: a pair of snub-nosed pliers, a needle-nosed type, common household pliers for shaping, and a very small pair of pliers for braiding work. Most pliers have toothed jaws, and visible marks will be left in the wire if they are used. Smooth pliers are best, but if you do not have any, wrap surgical tape around the household pliers.

Occasionally you might need an inexpensive hacksaw for cutting and a vise to hold the wire when you are bending forms. If an item has many curves you might want to make a homemade jig on which to bend wire (see photo for jig details).

Many of the projects in this book use a form of braiding (twisting, coiling, and so forth) to hold joints together. To further ensure a solid union, solder is used as well. Both techniques can be learned without much trouble. It takes only a little patience and practice.

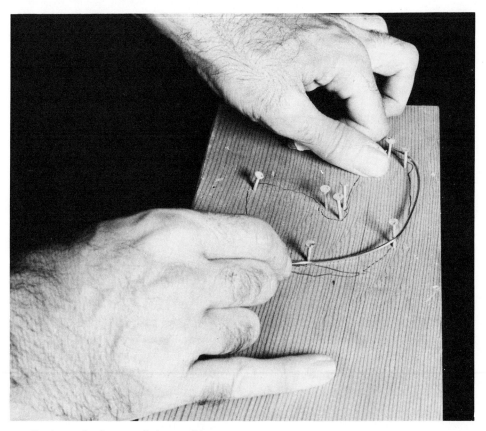

A jig is a device used in making a specific shape; nails are put into a board and wires wrapped around the nails. This jig was for a butterfly wing.

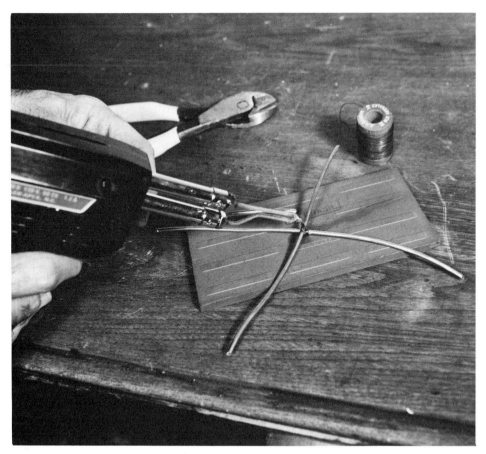

Using a soldering gun, two wires are crossed; flux-core wire was used and heat was applied with gun to join the wires.

Soldering

Soldering is a word used to denote the joining of metal parts by melting another metal (solder) into the gap between the parts to be joined. The solder must fill the gap and adhere to both pieces of wire. Since wire has oils and dirt that you cannot see, the wires to be soldered must be absolutely clean. A material called flux must be used to help melt the solder so it can flow properly onto the workpiece. In Chapter 4 you will find a complete discussion on soldering and how to do it.

Soldering Tools.   There are several ways to solder metals; but generally when soldering small works you should use an electric soldering iron or gun (the gun is more convenient because it has a trigger handle). Soldering irons and guns are available with heating elements ranging from 50 to 125 watts. The heating tip of the iron carries heat

Here flux-core wire is applied with soldering gun heat to join two wires. Note the brick used as work surface.

from the shank down to the work; the tip is usually made of copper, which conducts heat easily. To help conduct heat, the tip is coated with a layer of solder or tin.

A soldering-iron tip is hot, not so hot as a flame but as hot as an electric iron. Thus, it is hot enough to burn you if it is accidentally touched. Remember that anything touched by the hot tip will be burned. Use suitable safety precautions as you do in handling any electric iron.

Soldering Torch.   Nowadays you can buy a soldering-torch kit. The torch solders with a flame and is used for the large pieces a soldering iron cannot handle. The torch heats directly by flame, or the flame may be used to heat a large copper tip. In any case, the torch is used in the same manner as a soldering iron. If you have a torch on hand, use it for our projects, but basically the soldering iron or gun is fine.

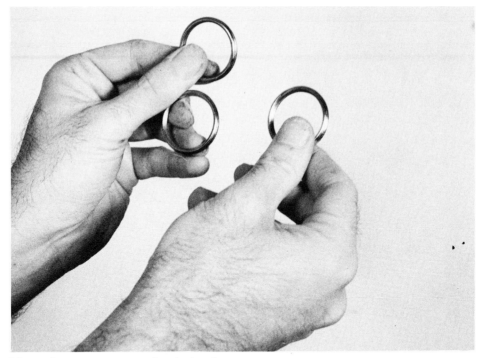

If you do not want to make circles for wire projects you can buy key rings and use the circles.

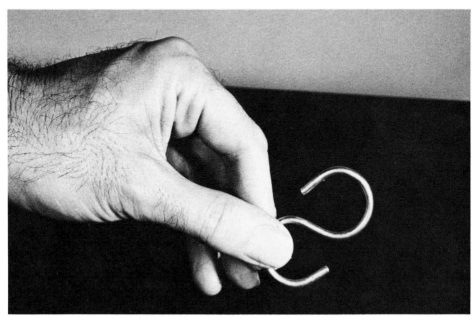

This is a commercial S-hook, available at hardware stores in many sizes; use these if you do not want to make your own.

Other Equipment

Solders and tools are easy to obtain, but a proper surface to work on needs some consideration. Solder collects in lumps on the underside of a work and adheres to any surface. To elevate the working area, set a cake-cooling rack on bricks and place a drip tray (an old pie plate, for example) underneath the rack. Put the item flat on the rack and work easily: excess solder will fall into the drip pan.

Keeping joints in firm contact until soldering is done can be tricky. You can use rubber bands, but they are not very dependable. Weights and bricks will help hold joints firmly, but the best way to keep joints together while you braid or solder them is to use clamps, electrical clips, or wooden clothespins. The clothespins seem to work best because they are lightweight, do not get hot, and can be moved quickly if necessary. However, they cannot be put into direct contact with flame. Plasticine or other claylike materials are also satisfactory for holding joints in place.

Shortcuts

Some of our projects call for S-shaped wire and some have small circles. We suggest you make your own shapes and circles, but for a shortcut you can buy S-hooks and use them for parts of the projects; S-hooks come in several sizes at hardware stores. Circles of wire are also available, and lamp and craft stores sell large circles which are specifically made for lamp work but which can be used for any circular shape specified in the working drawings.

The advantage of these shortcuts is that they save you time and bending, so you might want to use them, at least to get started. Later, however, you will probably want to fashion your own pieces since you have wire on hand.

2 Working with Wire

Since wire is essentially flat and straight, you have to curve and form and solder and tie and glue it to turn it into a finished product. In this chapter we really look into the methods and ways of shaping wire, and we discuss shapes so you can learn to make the objects. In Chapters 5 and 6 we will tell you actually how to make the items by using the many shaping methods described here.

Shaping Wire

Shaping the wire is probably the most difficult part of making any wire object (soldering and tying are fairly easy). The appearance of the final piece itself depends on how well you shape the wire. Note that

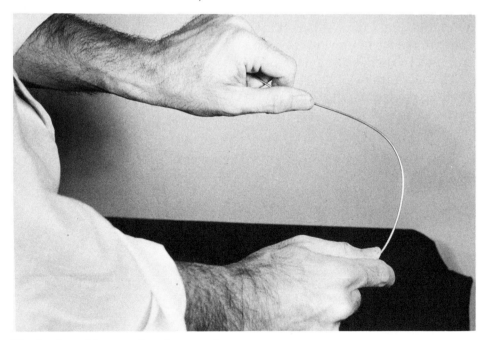

Work wire with your thumbs to make shapes as shown here.

Shaping Wire

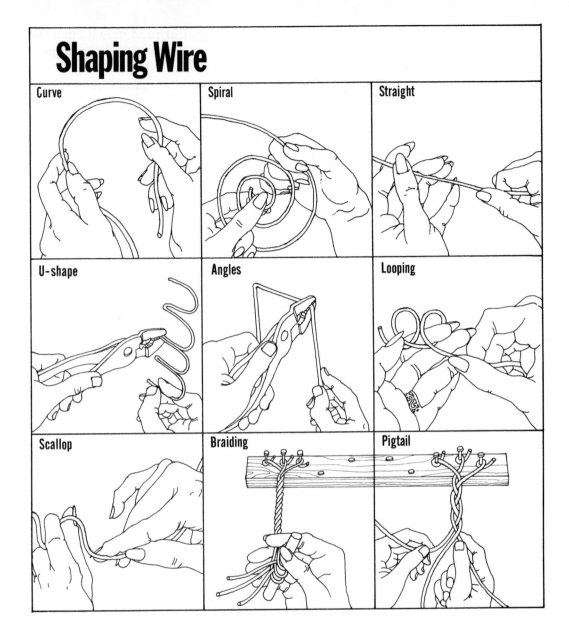

Curve

Spiral

Straight

U-shape

Angles

Looping

Scallop

Braiding

Pigtail

your first attempts probably will be less than desirable, but, of course, with practice you will improve. First try to make a curve from 16g wire. You may find that it is not as easy as you thought because wire, like paint strokes, shows any reworking. Thus, the shaping must be final on the first attempt. It must be smooth and without kinks or bends. Altering the wire with jerks produces angular and unsatisfactory results.

Curves.   A curve is basic to many of the designs — bowl and tray, for example — so learn this shape first. To make a smooth curve, grip one end of the wire securely with pliers. Hold the other end of the wire at least 12 inches away from you, and swing it around slowly; use the original curve of the wire as it comes off the coil. Now, with your fingers and thumbs, stroke along the wire and ease it into the exact curve you want. Use the ball of your thumb to create the final curve, and then cut a small part of the curve with just the right arc to it.

S-Shape.   Decorative and graceful, the S-shape is an easy one to make. Bend and work the piece of wire into the S-shape, using pliers. If many S-shapes are needed it is best to make a jig so each S will be similar in shape (see photo of jig in Chapter 1).

Circles.   Making a circle from a straight piece of wire seems like magic; actually, it is easy to do. Cut the length of wire from the coil. Curve the wire with your thumbs as described previously, grasping the two ends when a circle is formed. Now overlap the ends so they are parallel to each other; tie with thin-gauge wire and solder. If a perfect circle is needed, bring the two end wires almost together; secure the circle in a vise or other holding device and apply solder.

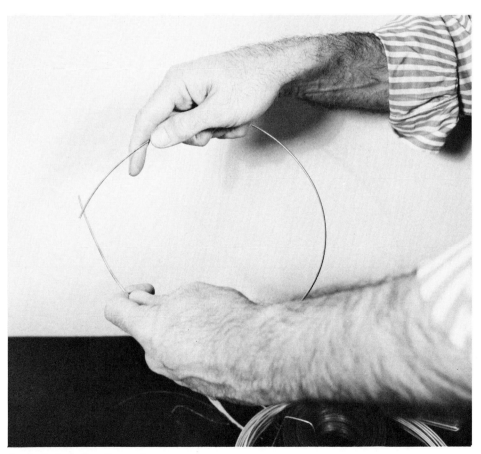

A circle is being formed.

Rectangles.   The basic procedure for making a rectangle is much the same as for making a circle except of course that the shape is rectangular. Securing the ends is the same. Either lace the ends together or have them almost touching and apply solder.

Spirals.   Spirals are decorative and form the body of bowls and baskets, trays and and shelving. To make a flat spiral, hold the tip of the wire with a pair of needle-nosed pliers, and wind slowly around as you did for curves, but create a flat disk as the circles get larger. Each curve of the spiral must be smooth, so stop and shape each one before going on to the next. If you try to recurve the spirals after the complete piece is made, the piece will look awful.

   Another way to make spirals is to form a small loop at the end of the wire. Hold this loop flat in the pliers, and work the wire round, coiling and bending it through the pliers that are gripping the center of the loop. Finally, you can make spirals by winding wire around a pencil or wooden dowel. Shape and firm the wire around the wooden object, one curve following another.

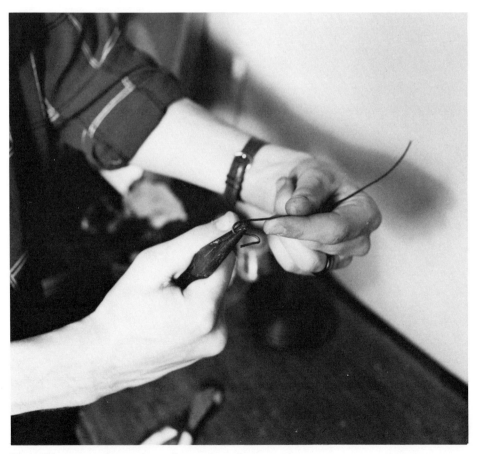

Use pliers to make various shapes in wire.

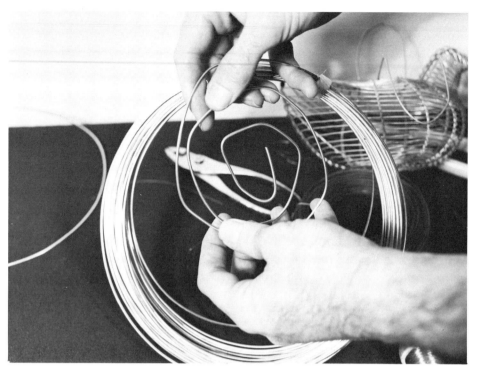

Starting a spiral pattern in wire.

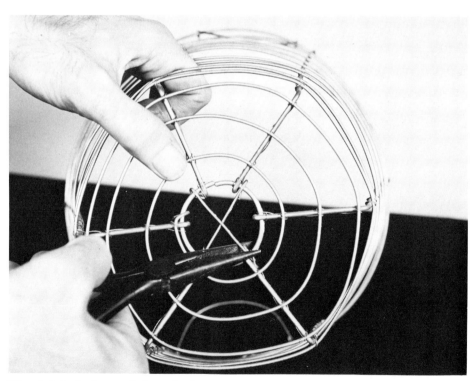

The finished shape of the spiral pattern.

Angles. You may think you can make a right angle in wire by merely kneading the wire with your hands, but this is not the case. For a really sharp and clean angle you need a table vise. Put the wire in the vise, and then bend the wire over a sharp corner (a block of wood works fine). If you do bend the wire with your hand, push the wire farther than the angle needed and then bring it back into the proper position.

Looping. To form a loop pattern, hold a piece of wire vertically, the lower end in the left hand. Now, start 2 inches up the wire, and bend the wire down over the right thumb into a loop. Work with the natural curve of the wire. Next, change hands; that is, hold the wire in your right hand and bend the wire down over your left thumb. You are thus making a loop in the opposite direction. As you keep changing hands, you should take the wire in front of each loop so the finished loops lie evenly. Loops are generally made in a continuous design and then cut into sections for use. Once the basic loop is made, you can pull it out to make loops smaller, or press it together to make a very close design.

Small spirals are made by looping wire over dowel.

Completed small spiral.

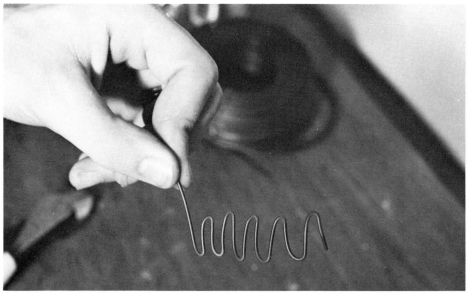

Simple snake-shape pattern.

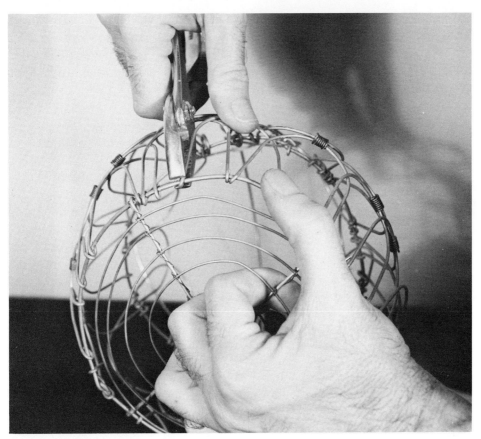

This basket shows the use of U-shapes.

U-Shape.   A U-shape is a conventional up-and-down pattern. Hold one end of a long piece of wire in your left hand. Working toward the right, bend the wire with the ball of your right finger, working the wire over the finger and up again around the top of the forefinger. Keep an even rhythm. The U-shape can be graded down to form large shapes or pulled out to create a somewhat zigzag effect.

Forging

Forging (shaping and flattening) is a wire process that creates unusual shapes and designs. To forge wire, lay the wire on a hard surface such as an anvil or vise top, and then hammer it flat. Steel hammers of different types are used to cold forge wire, and it is not something you can do in a moment, like bending wire. Thus forging requires some expertise.

Start by hammering the wire gradually; when the wire is the desired flatness, stop — too much hammering can ruin the total effect. The amount of hammering and time is dictated by the type of wire used. Wires of different metals have different malleability, so experiment a bit before doing an actual piece. Usually, forged wire is then annealed to bring it back to shape, but this is generally not necessary unless you are making fine jewelry.

Filing/Sanding

I cannot stress this important part of wire working too much. Whenever you are joining wires in an item that will have to take weight, be sure to file the crossing joints with a carpenter's file so the solder has a surface to grasp. The filing does not have to be extensive, just a run or two with the file at juncture points. You can also use emery sandpaper to create an abrasive surface.

Filigree pattern.

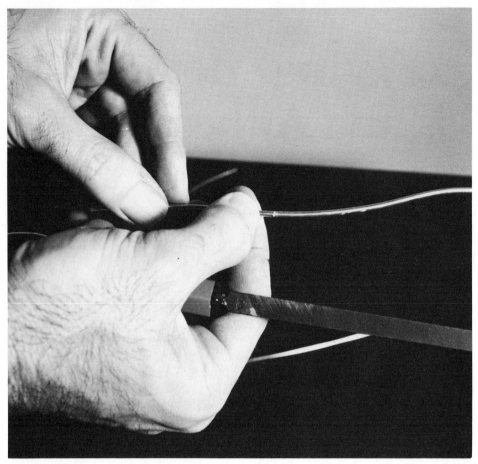

Making a file cut where wire will be placed for a joint.

3 Tying Methods and Adhesives

This chapter presents various methods of joining wires together without using solder, by tying them or by using adhesives.

Joining Methods

The principle of tying is that, although the wires are secured, they also give under weight and in so doing create even more strength. For example, a tied basket when empty is secure, but when you put apples or vegetables into the container, the weight further tightens the ties, creating a very solid receptacle. The wire chairs made in the 1920s worked on the principle of wire tying; these chairs had no soldered unions but relied on a person's weight to make them sturdy.

Tying methods include coiling, looping, braiding, lacing, crimping, twisting, crocheting, and weaving. All involve securing one strand of wire to another. It is important that you spend a good deal of time with this chapter and study the various drawings, because they are the key to successful wire working without using solder. As mentioned, when properly done, tied wire pieces can have more strength than soldered ones. And as a further advantage, a tied container has a hand-hewed look that is attractive and distinctive.

Like basket making or embroidery, wire tying keeps the fingers moving and the mind going because there are endless variations on knots, braiding, and "stitches." The difference between wirecraft and embroidery is that in embroidery you use a needle; in wirecraft you use small pliers as an extension of your hands. At first some of the processes may seem difficult, but they are not. You just have to get used to using wire instead of yarn or grass fiber.

One reminder: In this chapter I use terms associated with basket making — braiding, weaving — but they should not be thought of as identical. The methods are similar in assemblage but different in terms of the materials. Yet wire, like grasses or reeds, is a flexible material, so with some modification the basketry methods can be used for wire. And in every instance, we include drawings to show you *exactly* the techniques suggested.

Coiling.   The coiling process has been used for centuries in basket making. This form offers strength, versatility, and the creation of sculptural forms quite akin to wire-making products. The coil is easy to make, and we show this method in two photographs. You can use two

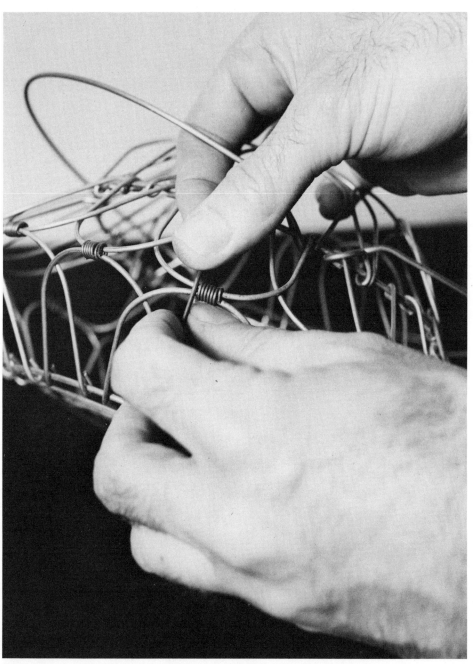

The coiling technique is used to secure wires.

Joining Methods

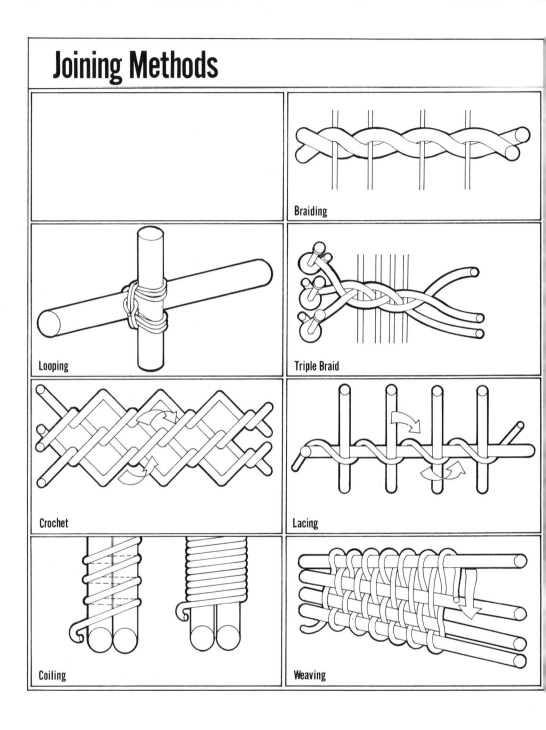

Braiding

Looping

Triple Braid

Crochet

Lacing

Coiling

Weaving

ways to tie the coil together: (1) a figure-eight stitch woven at every union, and (2) a lazy stitch that simply loops around each union.

Looping. The technique of looping is closely akin to coiling. The difference is that, with looping, the shape itself is used as a tying method and the wires are close together. Think of a straight piece of wire you want to join to another piece of wire. By looping another wire around the two wires you can fasten the wires together securely.

Crimping. If there is one technique you must learn to do successfully with wirecraft it is crimping, which means forming a U-shape at one end of a wire to fasten onto another wire. Crimping is a superior holding method, eliminates a great deal of soldering, and has a hand-hewed look. The end of the wire is secured around a vertical member and crimped down with blunt-nosed pliers. Crimping takes time, practice, and a strong hand; but with some experience you will find that it comes naturally and can be used for fastening wires in an endless variety of designs.

Study the drawings of items in this book carefully to see the many techniques of crimping and their successful application.

Lacing (Wrapping). Lacing is an over-and-under weaving technique; wire is put over and under another wire and laced into a quasi-coil shape. Wire lacing is essential in many pieces because it holds the pieces together, and it is sometimes stronger than soldered joints.

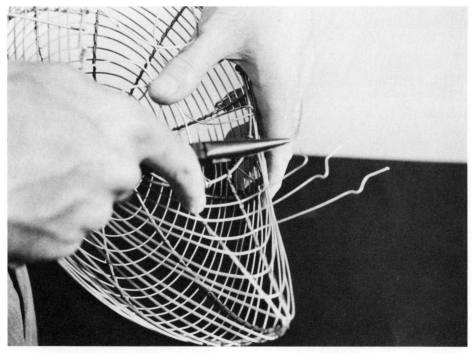

*The long wires are joined to the short
wires in this wire basket by lacing.*

Joining Methods

Twisting

Crimping

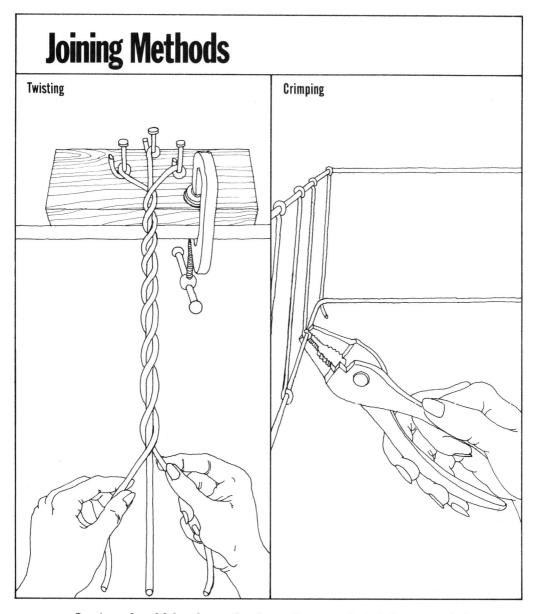

Lacing should be done slowly and secured tightly around the wires to be joined. Start one end of laced wire by making a small U-shaped hook, to give the wire a start. Holding the wire with your thumb just leads to trouble, so be sure to start one end securely and then gently and slowly twist the wires around each succeeding joint. Sometimes a second layer is needed to really hold pieces together.

In some cases lacing can actually be tied as string. The tying method is more secure than the twisting process but requires a rather thin wire. Tie the wire as you would string, and use several lengths, tying each one to make a secure joint. When all the ends are tied, clip off excess wire.

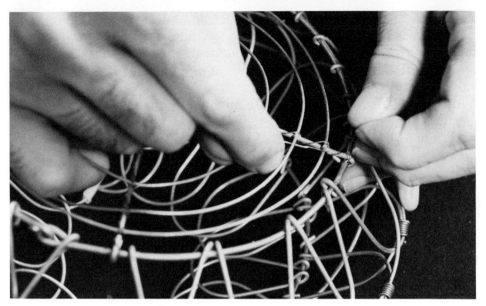

Another example of lacing joints together.

Wires are twisted to join the four verticals.

Twisting. A common method of joining wire, twisting is easily done by hand or with a mechanical aid like a vise. Twisted wire can also be used for strength, that is, one wire twisted onto another one for added diameter and durability. The hand method is necessary when using twisted wires for joining; the mechanical method can be used for decorative uses of wire. To use a vise, loop wires around a wooden dowel and secure the ends in a vise. The dowel gives you the needed leverage.

Braiding.   Braiding, similar to twisting, is like braiding hair. The braid may take on many shapes or styles: single, double, or triple. You can make strands of braided wire and attach them to objects for handsome effects, or use the hand-braiding process to join wires.

Weaving.   This process is vitally important in wire work and is similar to the weaving process used with fibers. The warp and weft of traditional weaving will be varied, but the final results are very similar to cloth weaving. Patterns are handsome, and woven wire is strong and often preferred to a soldered object. Three-dimensional forms can be created by weaving wires on a central axis. You can do most wire weaving with your hands or with small blunt-nosed pliers.

Crocheting.   It is hard to imagine, but you can crochet thin wire as you do yarn. It does take some practice, but after you have mastered braiding and other tying techniques, you might want to try crocheting because it creates handsome patterns. Many of the vegetable-basket–type strainers are crocheted. Fine wire can be looped and pulled through with a standard crochet needle to make crochet-type patterns. The process is almost identical to standard crocheting, but with wire, which cannot find a consistent shape by itself, you must form each loop to the proper pattern.

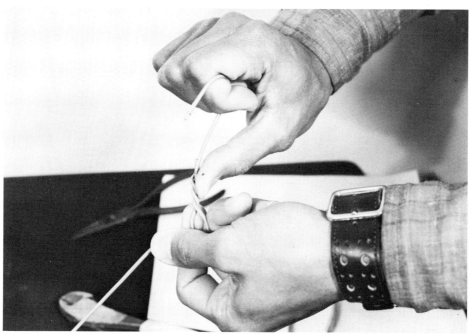

This coat-hanger top is an example of how braiding is used to join two wires.

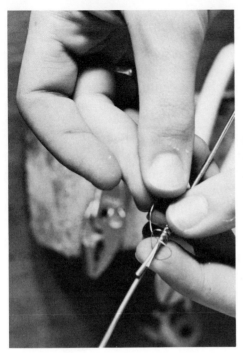

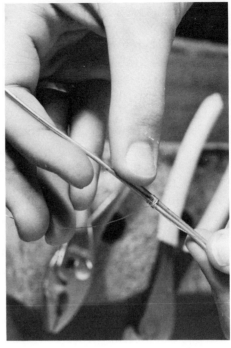

Joining wires by simple looping.

Joining wire by using the simple coil pattern.

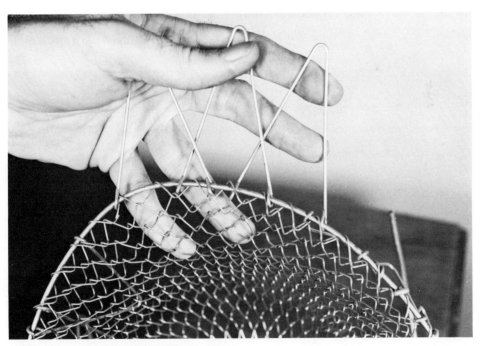

A commercial salad basket uses the crocheting technique of tying.

Adhesives

Besides tying methods, wire can be joined with adhesives. Cold (liquid) solders are applied without heat, which is convenient, but they are not particularly strong and so should be used only for light work. The basic standard household glues (white glues) are good only for light work.

The two-part epoxy cements are much stronger than cold solder and have a variety of uses in wire work. The epoxies are mixed first and then applied to clean wire. Some of the epoxies set quickly, while others take much longer to harden. Most have to be clamped together so they bond joints securely. Be careful not to cement the clamp!

Bonding with epoxy resins requires that the surfaces of the wires be absolutely free of dirt and grease. Rub the parts to be joined several times with sandpaper or emery board so they are slightly abrasive. Then wash the wires with detergent to remove grease, rinse the wires in warm water, and dry thoroughly. Follow the manufacturer's directions for mixing the hardener and the resin. Apply the resin in dabs — never too much — and clamp pieces together so they will not move during the setting process. (But do not clamp so tightly that epoxy is squeezed out of the touching surfaces.) Lay the work aside and let it set completely.

Because there are several good adhesives on the market, be sure to read all directions carefully: there are variations on how to use the products.

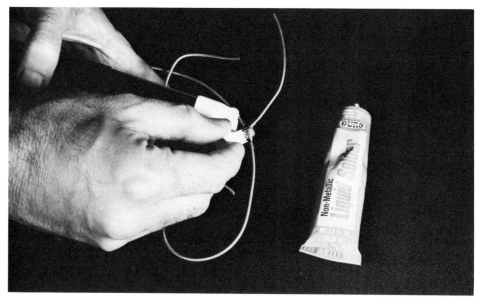

Liquid solder is used to help secure joints.

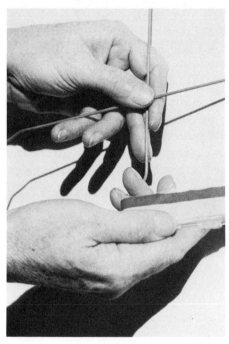

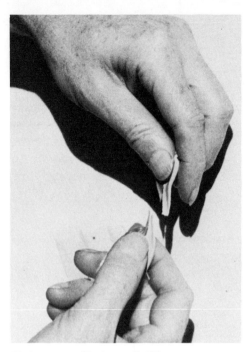

E–Pox–E Ribbon will be used to "solder" these joints.

Take a small piece of ribbon . . .

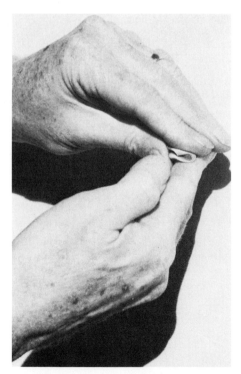

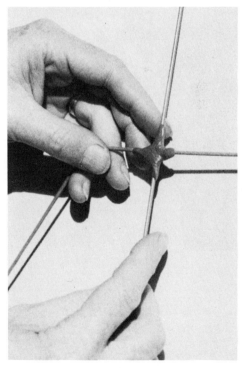

Crumble and mix in your hand until the material turns uniformly green.

Mold the material around the joint as shown and let it dry for two hours.

One epoxy product I want to mention specifically, called E–Pox–E Ribbon, is so simple to use and so suitable for holding wire joints, that it must be recommended. This is a non-toxic epoxy manufactured by Duro. The application is simple: merely remove a small piece of the ribbon, which is yellow and blue; crumble and roll it in your hands until it is uniformly green. It is now ready for use. Wrap and mold the material around a joint; within two hours it is set and within 12 hours it is as hard as steel. The joint cannot be pulled apart.

If soldering is too time consuming and tying too tricky, by all means use this epoxy. It dries to a dull green color, but this is no disadvantage because you can always paint the finished objects or merely touch up the joints.

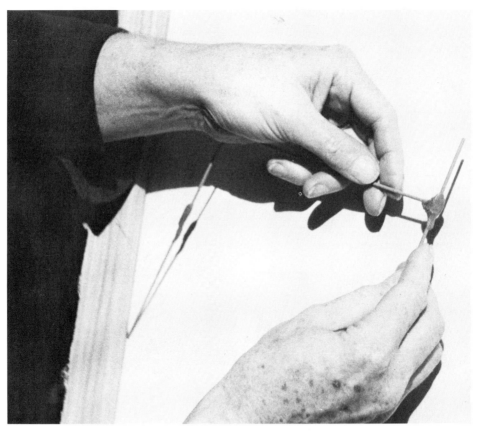

Using ribbon putty for a "T" connection.

4 Soldering

Soldering is the accepted joining method for wire because it joins securely, even when subjected to physical stress and the expansion of the wire itself from heat and cold. Soldering can be done with an inexpensive iron or gun.

Solder can be used to join almost any metals, except aluminum and chromium, which have to be welded. For wire joints we use what is called a soft solder, that is, a solder composed of a soft metal, like tin or lead. (Hard solder is used for other types of metal joining.) Whenever you solder wires together it is vital that they be held in some manner: perhaps in a vise, or simply with Scotch tape wrapped around the two wires. The wires must be in contact somehow while the soldering is done. You can also loop thin wire around the pieces to be soldered and then apply solder.

A spool of core solder or flux solder, which has both solder and flux, for one-step soldering. Solder also comes in rod form as shown in rear.

Cleaning Wire

If you fail to solder correctly, you probably have not cleaned the wire thoroughly. The joint areas of the wires must be totally free of the oils, grease, and dirt that are on all wires. If these residues are left on the wires to be joined, the solder will ball up and create havoc rather than flowing smoothly into the joint. Solder adheres by forming an alloy with the wire; this alloy will not form if there is an oxide, film, rust, or tarnish.

Clean the wire with emery cloth, steel wool, or a file. When the wire is clean, it should be joined together as closely as possible — if there are large gaps between the wires to be joined, the solder cannot span the space. You can prejoin wire by braiding with a soft 20g wire, or use clothespins, rubber bands, or any devices that will keep the wires touching.

To clean wires thoroughly where joints are to be made you can use a product called tinners fluid.

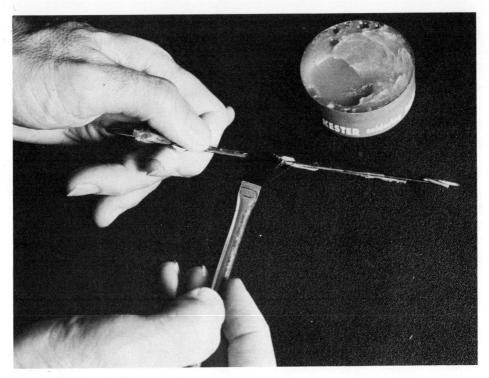

Flux being applied separately to two pieces of wire to be soldered.

Solders and Fluxes

Solders are either soft (made of tin and lead), with a low melting point of 400° to 700°F, or hard (made of silver, copper, and zinc), with an average melting point of 1350°F. Hard solder, also called silver solder, is usually used for jewelry work or with silver and copper wire. Since we do not use silver wire in any of our projects hard solder is not necessary. Remember that the term "soft solder" denotes melting at a lower temperature than hard solder; it does *not* mean it is softer or inferior.

Soft solder adheres by an intermetallic solution that it forms with the wire at low temperatures. It is thus a chemical attachment process. Generally, the most commonly used type of soft solder is 50 percent tin and 50 percent lead and is the kind we used for many projects. Soft solder is available in wire form, ribbons, solid bars, foils, powders, and paste.

Fluxes are used with solder because when fluxes are heated they become slightly acid and molten and dissolve any tarnish or rust on the wire.

There are two basic fluxes: salt or a mixture of acid and resin. The salt flux is rather corrosive and leaves some residue that can be removed by either washing after the joint is made or by burning while the joint is hot. The resin-type flux is used for electrical work and is beyond our scope here.

To avoid your having to use flux and solder separately, fluxes are usually combined with solder and sold as flux-cored solder wire. This is a solid wire with several cores of flux inside it. This dual product ensures enough solder and flux for rapid flow on the work. Flux-core wire is the easiest type of solder to use for our purposes because it combines the flux and solder for one-step application and comes in $\frac{1}{8}$-, $\frac{3}{32}$-, and $\frac{1}{16}$-inch diameters. Regular-size flux core of $\frac{1}{8}$ inch is usually used for craft work. Flux is also available in solid or liquid forms. With these forms application involves two steps: applying the flux and then soldering.

Only soft solder has a melting point low enough so it can be used with soldering irons and guns; other solders require a propane torch.

Flux-core solder being applied with soldering gun.

Completing the joint with heat from gun.

Tape is used to hold wires together
before they are soldered.

48

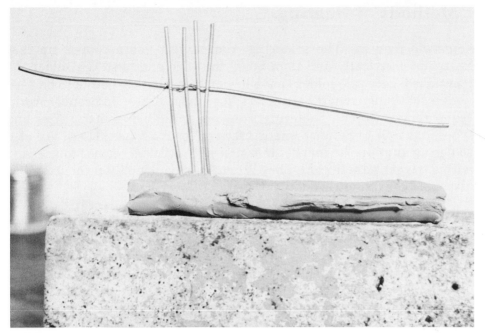

Floral clay comes in handy to hold pieces steady while soldering.

Soldering with an Iron

Be sure to use a soldering iron or gun that has a tip large enough to cover the joint. Most electric irons require a few minutes to heat up. When using flux-core solder wire, use the side of the iron and the heat of the metal to do the melting. It is very important to apply the core solder to the work and then touch the soldering iron to the solder to melt it. This allows the solder and the flux to carry the heat from the soldering tip to the joint. (Rubbing the iron over the joint may be necessary to help spread the heat of the iron.) If you apply the flux-core solder to the tip of the soldering iron, the solder will melt too quickly. If you apply the heated iron to the joint itself, it will oxidize the union and make it more difficult to solder.

While the joint is heating, the solder will be of a spongy consistency, but suddenly it will turn bright and fluid and start to flow a few seconds after heating, so be prepared. This flow is what you want to fully penetrate the joint and fill the gap. If you wait too long, both the flux and the solder will become too hot and will burn, in which case you will have to push more core solder wire under the iron.

When the joint looks as if it is coated with solder, remove the iron and let the joint cool. Hang up the hot iron or unplug it, and be sure to set it out of the way while it cools. All soldering irons or guns should be "tinned" so the solder flows easily.

Methods of Heating

Soldering Iron.   The soldering iron or gun has a copper tip that heats up electrically and then heats the wire ends and the solder. As mentioned, only soft solders have low enough heating points to be used with a soldering iron; other solders (for silver, brass, and copper work) require flame (torch). Soldering irons are available in many sizes and types, but a 6- to 8-ounce one is efficient for craft use. There are also soldering guns on the market that are more efficient, easier to use, and with a trigger handle grip. They are more expensive than the irons but also more convenient.

Soldering with a Propane Torch.   The propane torch is available in small, hand-held, easy-to-use models and works beautifully for soldering wires. The torch is easy to use because the heat can be regulated, and the flame heats faster and covers a larger area than a soldering gun. When starting a torch always hold the nozzle away from you. Carefully follow the instructions that come with the torch.

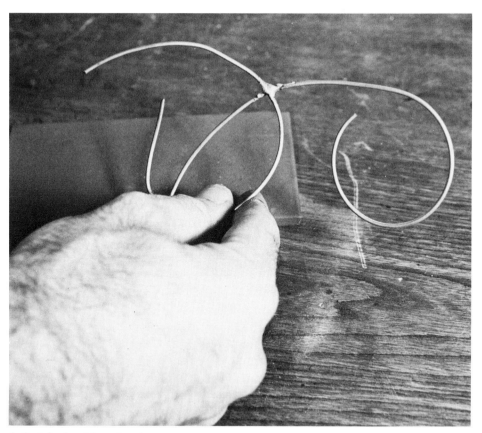

A finished soldered union.

Holding (Clamping)

No matter which soldering process you use, holding the pieces securely in place is half the battle. The crossing pieces or touching parts
must be in exactly the right place to make it all work. Flat objects are
the easiest to hold for soldering because they can be laid over a rack
and held with weights, clamps, clothespins, or screw clips. As long as
the intersections are in close contact there is little difficulty.

For pieces that must be held in other than a flat position, make a
base of clay or some other soft material that will hold the item upright
while you work on it. A wooden base with suitable holes is also satisfactory.

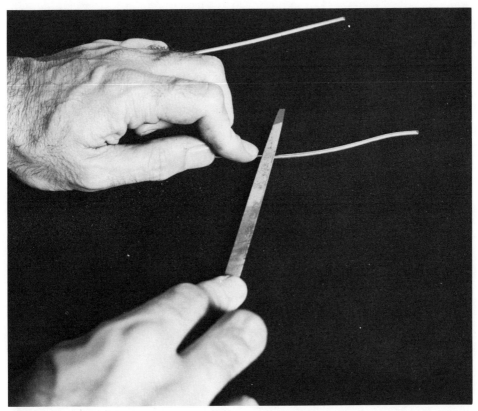

*File cut is made where wire is to be
joined and soldered.*

5 Coat-hanger Wire Projects

Probably the easiest and least expensive way to get started in wirecraft is to use wire coat hangers. The coat hanger is usually made of 16g wire, which is neither too thick nor too thin for working. To start, try to shape and bend a hanger into a straight piece. Use your hands and pliers, and then hammer the wire on a wooden block to make it straight. Do not try to use the hook and braiding because it is just too much trouble to unwind the hook for the additional few inches. Instead, snip the wire at one end, below the hook, and then at the other end, below the braiding. This gives you approximately 32 inches of straightened wire.

Cutting coat-hanger wire to make circle.

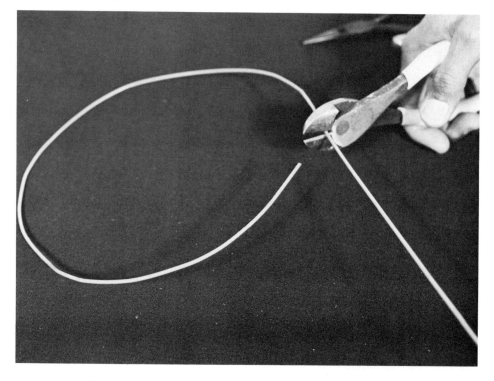

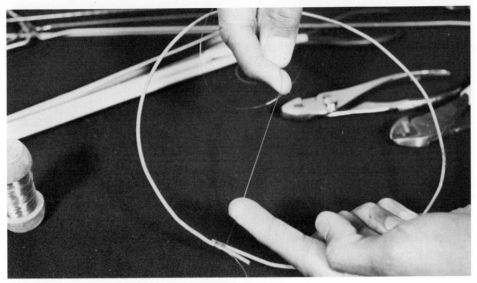

Forming a circle using the tie method.

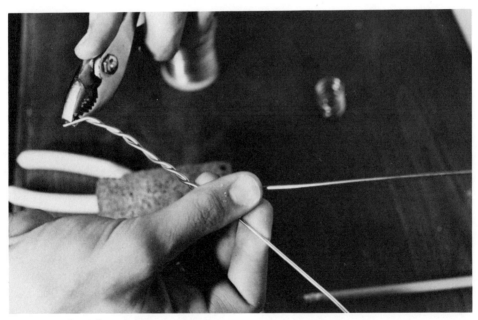

You can braid coat-hanger wire to give the wire double strength.

Some of the things you can make from salvaged coat-hanger wire are a lampshade frame, a sign holder, a candle snuffer, and a wall plaque — for example, a goldfish. The difference between using purchased wire and coat hangers (aside from the cost), is the time involved in straightening and cutting the hangers.

When using coat hangers for projects, cut them as previously described. Now put masking tape on the ends to avoid scratching yourself. Work with pliers and your fingers, and you might want to wear gloves. If you use painted hangers, be sure to file off the paint if you intend to solder at union joints.

Goldfish Wall Plaque

Following the pattern, make a drawing of all the pieces of the goldfish; you can make it any size you like. After you have cut out the pieces, arrange the wires on the drawing. This will act as a guide as you follow the assembly directions.

Solder the body (A) to make a circle. Solder the three pieces of tail wire (D) to the body. Solder the fins (B) and (C) to the body. Now solder the gills (E) and the eye (F) to the body. Last of all, solder the mouth (G) in place.

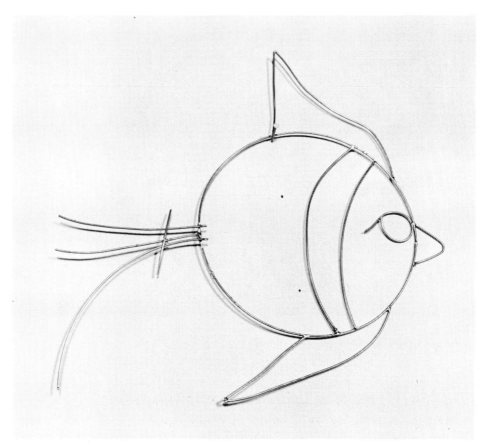

Goldfish

Goldfish

Note: Arrows indicate solder points

LETTER	DESCRIPTION
A	Circle — 16 gauge (coat hanger wire)
B	Bottom Fin — 16 gauge
C	Top Fin — 16 gauge
D	Tail Wires — 16 gauge
E	Gills — 16 gauge
F	Eye — 16 gauge
G	Mouth — 16 gauge

You can use the goldfish as a wall sculpture or hang it with mono-filament wire from a nail in the ceiling to make it into a mobile. Naturally, a spray of gold paint is ideal for a goldfish.

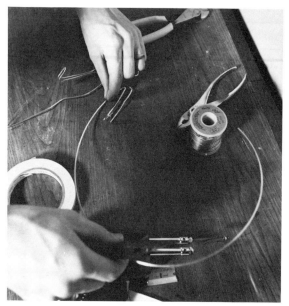

Starting the goldfish wall sculpture.

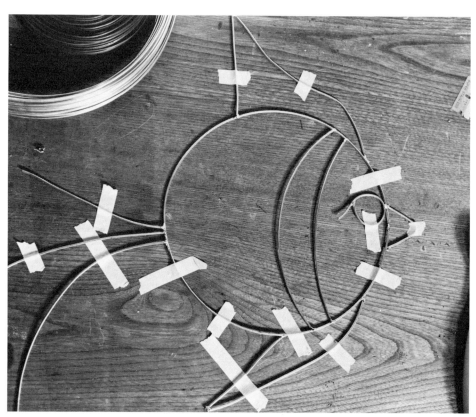

Masking tape is useful for holding pieces in place before soldering.

56

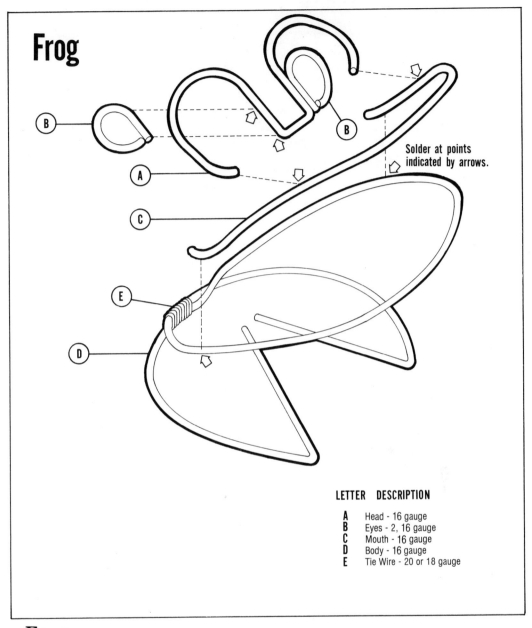

Frog

An easy accent for a table or desk is a freeform frog. Following the pattern, bend the wire for the body into shape with your thumbs. If the first attempt is not successful, try again; it takes a little expertise. When you have the form (D), braid at point E to hold the body together. For the mouth, form wire C and solder where indicated. To make the head (A), form the wire as shown and attach the eyes (B) to the head piece. Solder this piece to wire C.

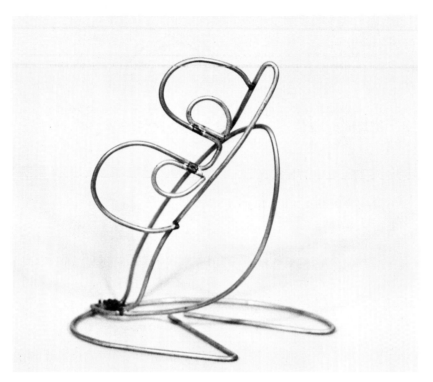

Frog

Sign Holder

A sign holder made from coat hangers can be a decorative piece for your desk or table or just a nameplate. It is a nice way of saying "I did it myself," since you simply cannot buy a sign holder.

Sign holder

Sign Holder

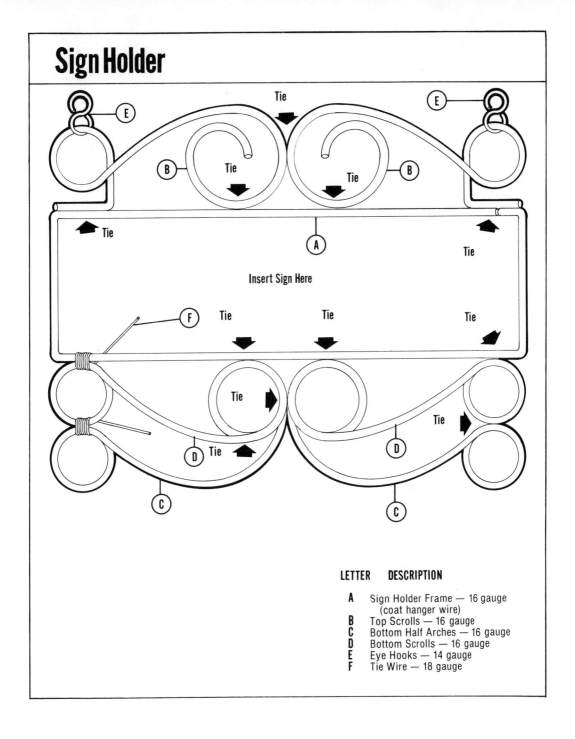

LETTER	DESCRIPTION
A	Sign Holder Frame — 16 gauge (coat hanger wire)
B	Top Scrolls — 16 gauge
C	Bottom Half Arches — 16 gauge
D	Bottom Scrolls — 16 gauge
E	Eye Hooks — 14 gauge
F	Tie Wire — 18 gauge

To make this sign holder, first form rectangular frame (A). Next, cut and shape two top scrolls (B) as shown, and tie them to the top of frame A. Now, cut two C and D wires and form them into scrolls. Tie C to D, and then tie D to A. Attach two hooks (E) to the top of B for hanging.

Lampshade

Why make a lampshade when you can buy one? Because lampshades are so expensive and this one will cost you pennies, or rather your old coat hangers. This is a simple lampshade to make, one that can be covered with parchment for a handsome item. Cut the basic frame (C), bending it as shown to form vertical members at top. Use two circles (A); fit and glue the bottom circle in place, and solder the top circle to the frame. To make the light bulb holder, form wires D as shown in the inset, and solder them to the bottom of circle A.

Cover the shade, using suitable parchment or other materials available at supply stores.

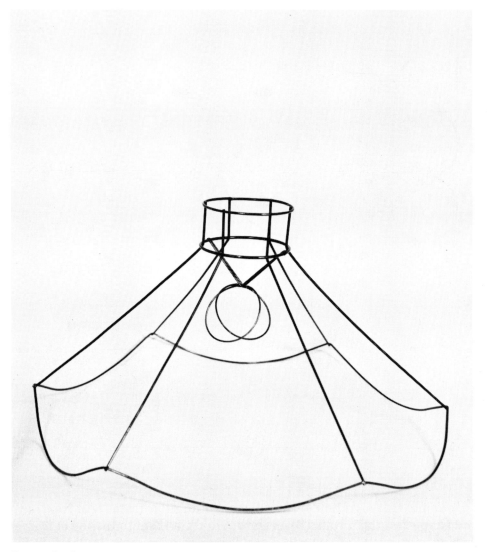

Lampshade

Lampshade

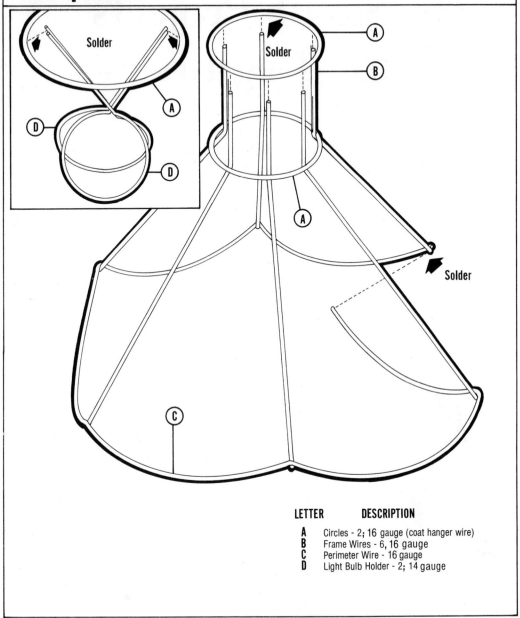

Solder

Solder

Solder

LETTER	DESCRIPTION
A	Circles - 2; 16 gauge (coat hanger wire)
B	Frame Wires - 6, 16 gauge
C	Perimeter Wire - 16 gauge
D	Light Bulb Holder - 2; 14 gauge

The coat-hanger projects in the last chapter are only a few of the things a beginner can make. Here are four more, each quite different, but none of them difficult.

Wall Candle Holder

This is a handsome simple design. First, shape the basic frame (B) as shown, soldering the ends together. Shape wire A to the contour of one

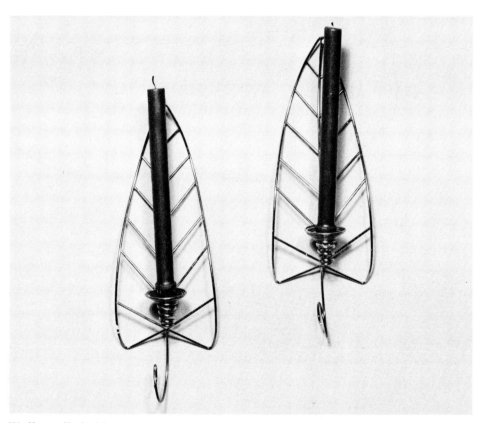

Wall candle holder

Wall Candle Holder

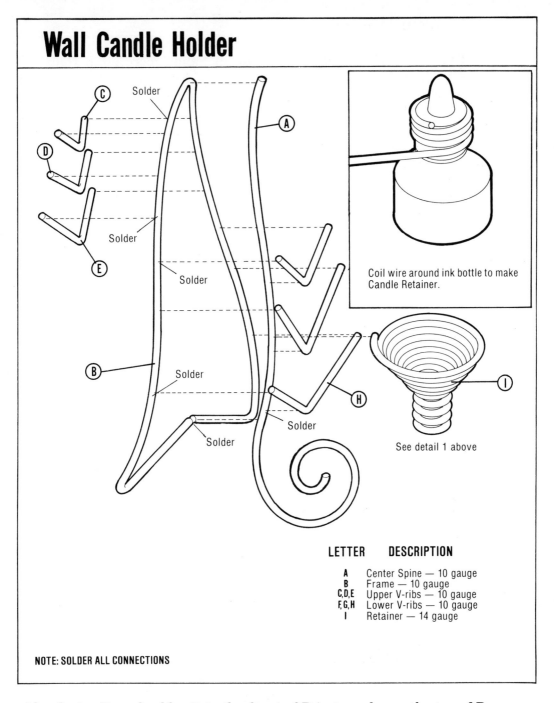

Solder

Coil wire around ink bottle to make Candle Retainer.

See detail 1 above

LETTER	DESCRIPTION
A	Center Spine — 10 gauge
B	Frame — 10 gauge
C,D,E	Upper V-ribs — 10 gauge
F,G,H	Lower V-ribs — 10 gauge
I	Retainer — 14 gauge

NOTE: SOLDER ALL CONNECTIONS

side of wire B, and solder it to the front of B in two places: the top of B and the soldered ends. Now make a series of V-shaped forms (CDE, FGH); solder CDE to the back of wire B, and solder wires FGH to the front of wires A and B. Solder the coiled wire (I), which will hold the candle, to the front of wire A. To make the coiled wire, see the inset.

This piece looks especially dramatic in gold or black.

Napkin Holder

This interesting holder will come in handy more often than you think, for both napkins and hand towels. First, form a rectangular frame (C) from 12g wire; solder the ends as shown. Next, form A and B wires into the shape shown, and attach them to the frame by braiding with 18g wire (E). Form legs (D), and attach them to the bottom of the frame with 18g tie wire (E). That's all there is to it. This project takes only a few minutes to make and is highly recommended for beginners.

Paint or spray the holder.

Napkin holder

Napkin Holder

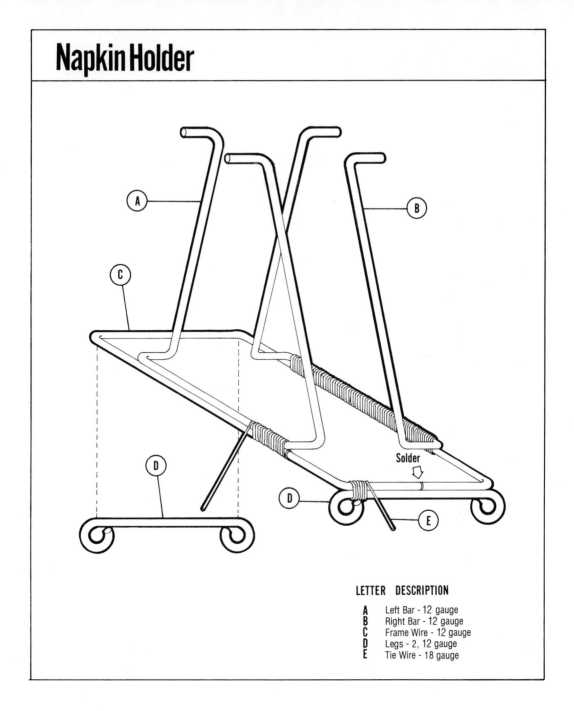

Solder

LETTER   DESCRIPTION

A	Left Bar - 12 gauge
B	Right Bar - 12 gauge
C	Frame Wire - 12 gauge
D	Legs - 2, 12 gauge
E	Tie Wire - 18 gauge

Candle Snuffer

This is a basic two-wire piece, with solder joints at various junctures. The leaves (C) and snuffer (E) are also soldered in finishing the project. First, shape and curve the stem wires A and B. Now cut out leaves from sheet metal (C) (see Chapter 1), and with pliers bend the base of each

Candle Snuffer

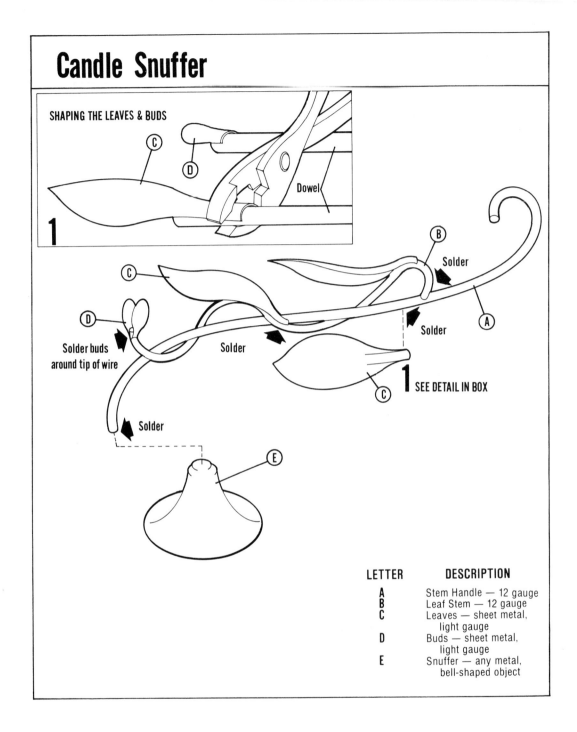

SHAPING THE LEAVES & BUDS

1

Dowel

B

Solder

C

Solder

A

D

Solder buds around tip of wire

Solder

C

Solder

1 SEE DETAIL IN BOX

Solder

E

LETTER	DESCRIPTION
A	Stem Handle — 12 gauge
B	Leaf Stem — 12 gauge
C	Leaves — sheet metal, light gauge
D	Buds — sheet metal, light gauge
E	Snuffer — any metal, bell-shaped object

leaf over a 12g dowel to ensure a secure connection to stem B. (See detail 1, where the sheet metal leaf [D] is formed over the dowel.) Solder each leaf in place, and solder the bell-nosed snuffer to the end of A as shown. (The snuffer can be any metal or bell-shaped object, or can be fashioned from sheet metal.)

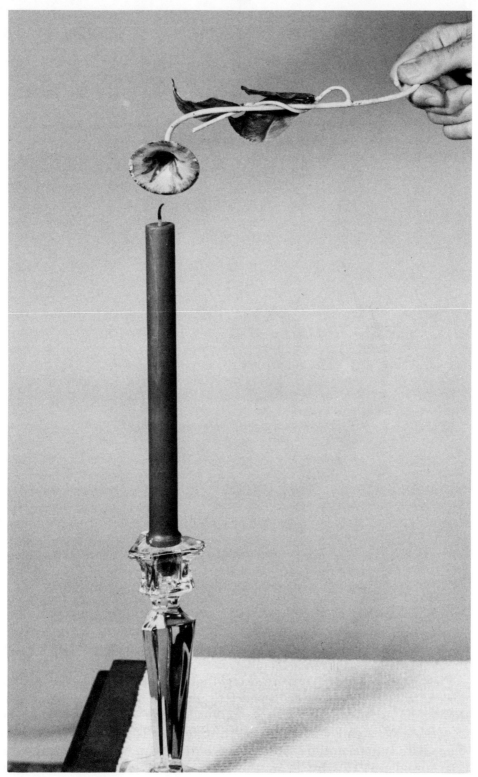

Candle snuffer

Swan Dish

This basic fruit bowl or decorative piece is made of 12g wire. It is essentially in three pieces, with parts E and F as an eye and a beak for the swan. The dish is made as follows:

First, solder the ends of wire A together to make a circle. Then cut a piece of wire mesh (H) (hardware cloth) approximately 2 inches wider than circle A. Solder the edges of this cut piece of wire mesh to the rim of wire A. Next, mold the wire mesh to form a bowl, as shown. Now, shape wire B to form the graceful lines of the swan body. Then cut wire C and solder it to wire B, at the tail end. Next, file ⅛ inch of the uppermost tip of wire E flat, and solder a small washer (F) to the end of

Swan Dish

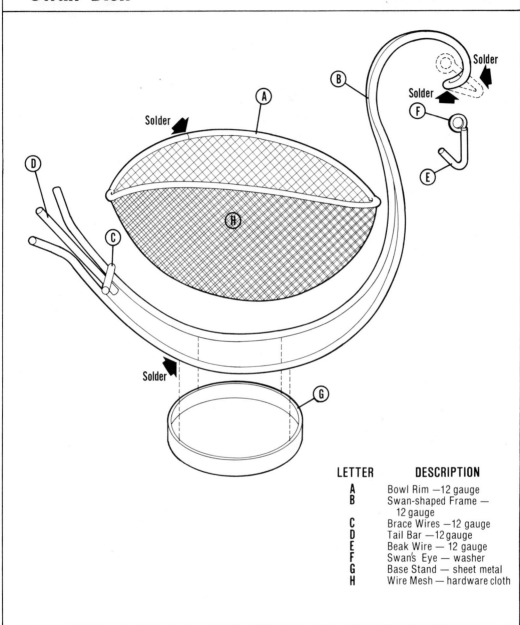

Solder

Solder

Solder

Solder

Solder

LETTER	DESCRIPTION
A	Bowl Rim —12 gauge
B	Swan-shaped Frame — 12 gauge
C	Brace Wires —12 gauge
D	Tail Bar —12 gauge
E	Beak Wire — 12 gauge
F	Swan's Eye — washer
G	Base Stand — sheet metal
H	Wire Mesh — hardware cloth

it. Solder E and F combined to the inside of the front end of wire B to make the eye and beak of the swan. Finally, form a circle from a strip of sheet metal to make the base (G), and solder this to the bottom of wire B.

This dish is finished in black paint (a bright color might be nice to match kitchen decor), but you can use any type of finishing.

Cup Holder

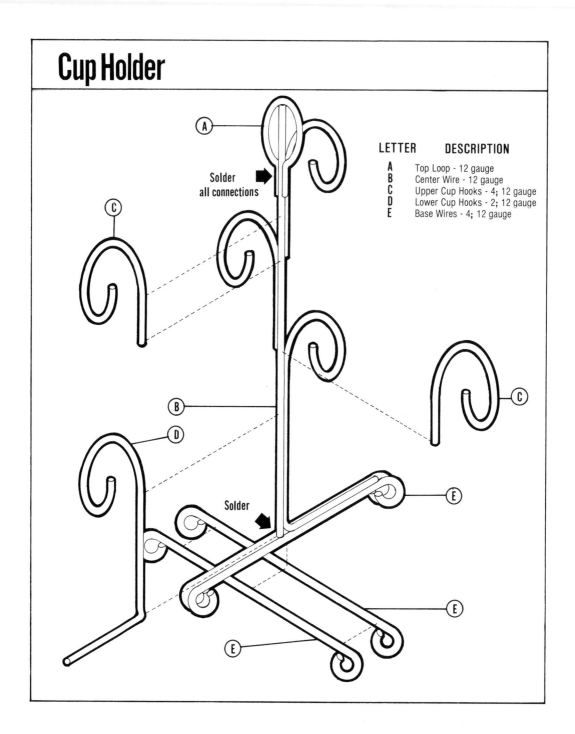

LETTER	DESCRIPTION
A	Top Loop - 12 gauge
B	Center Wire - 12 gauge
C	Upper Cup Hooks - 4; 12 gauge
D	Lower Cup Hooks - 2; 12 gauge
E	Base Wires - 4; 12 gauge

Solder all connections

Solder

Cup Holder

Here is something for the kitchen and a space saver as well. The cup holder holds six or twelve cups (two to a ring); and the basic construction is easy. First, form the top loop (A) and solder it to wire B, which is the central support. Now form four wires (C) and two wires (D) by bending. Solder the C and D wires to B. Next, form four wires (E) for the base, as shown. Finally, solder all junction points between E and B. The critical part in this project is attaching B to E, so be sure the soldered joint is secure enough to hold the weight of the cup hooks.

 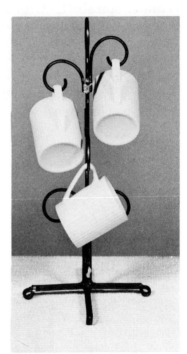

Cup holder

Pencil/Pen Holder

An excellent project for the beginner, and a handy desk gadget, the pencil/pen holder uses coiled wire as holders soldered to a wire frame. The basic construction is simple. Form two U-shaped wires (A), and solder three wires (B) to the top of A, as shown. Now attach the wire retainer spirals (C) with solder. (To make the wire spirals, form wire over the pointed end of a dowel, as shown in the inset.) Solder or glue the *sides* of the coils, as shown.

If you want to protect the wires from scratching your desk, put felt at the bottom of A. The size of the pen and pencil holder can be of any dimension to fit your needs, and you can use as many spirals to hold pencils as you desire.

Pen/Pencil holder

Pencil/Pen Holder

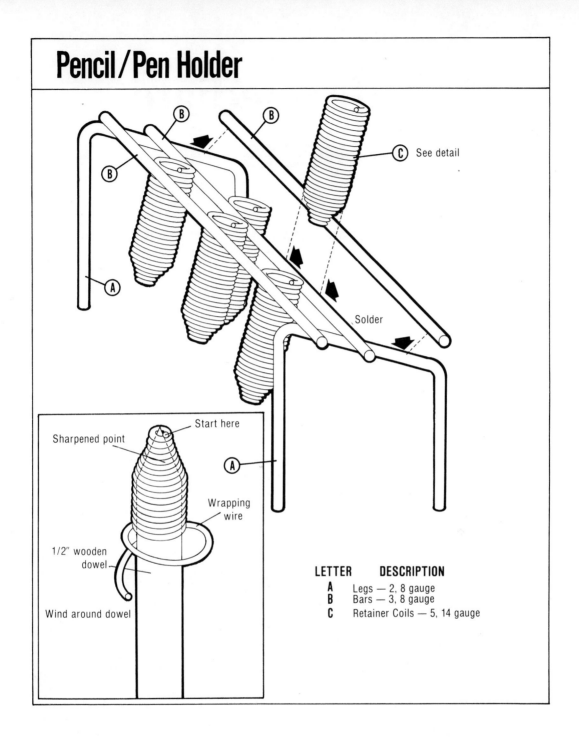

See detail

Solder

Start here

Sharpened point

Wrapping wire

1/2" wooden dowel

Wind around dowel

LETTER	DESCRIPTION
A	Legs — 2, 8 gauge
B	Bars — 3, 8 gauge
C	Retainer Coils — 5, 14 gauge

7 Intermediate Projects

The following projects are slightly more difficult, but if you have completed several of the previous items, these should present no trouble.

On the drawings, we have included the gauge of wire we used; in some cases, another gauge can be substituted. Most of the projects were made of galvanized wire. In general, joints are soldered; however, the wire baskets, plate rack, and the human form are executed without any soldering or tying methods.

No dimensions are given. The size you decide upon will depend on your use for an item.

Baskets

Wire baskets serve a multitude of uses — to hold bread or eggs, to hang plants in, to hold soap, or just as handsome sculptural accents in a kitchen or bathroom. None of the baskets is difficult, but all do require some time and patience to put together. The bread basket is the hardest.

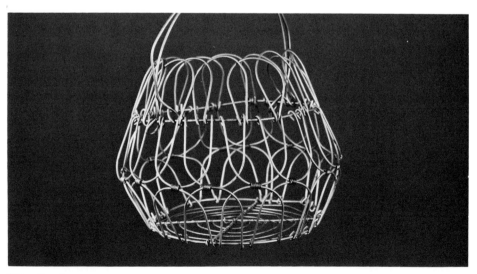

Wire Basket

Wire Basket: Assembly

Wire Basket.   This folding wire basket can be used for eggs, for drying salad greens, or as an ornament in the kitchen. The basket is composed of a series of U-shaped wires crimped at the edges (C and E). The bottom of the basket consists of formed spiral wires (H) with cross braces (F). Tie securely (see photo). The top circle (B) and bottom circle (G) are interlocked at ends (see drawing in Chapter 2). The handle (A) is crimped to attach to circle B. This project uses no solder but does take some expertise. Try it only if you have mastered the previous projects.

Bread (or Fruit) Basket.   This decorative wire basket is done with a series of S-shapes (A). Bend your own on a jig or buy ready-made S-forms. Wires B and C are the top and bottom frames; both of these wires are soldered midpoint to make a rectangle. The S-shapes are soldered or tied into position with tie wire (D). The construction is basically simple once all S-shapes are made. Spray the bread or fruit basket with black paint for a handsome piece. Total cost: $2.

Bread basket

Bread Basket

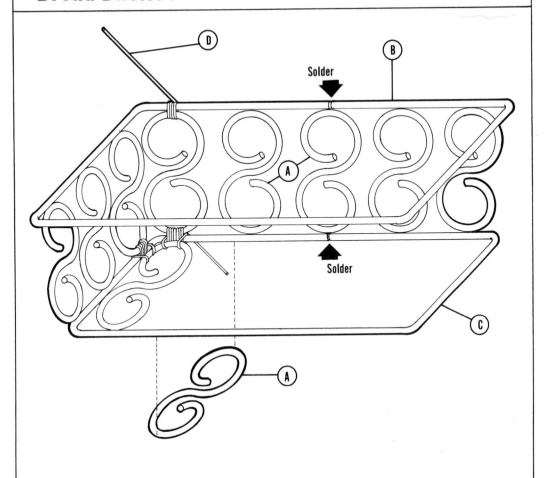

Solder

Solder

LETTER DESCRIPTION

A   Scrolls — 10 gauge
B   Top Frame — 10 gauge
C   Bottom Frame — 10 gauge
D   Tie Wire — 18 gauge

77

Table Tray

Table Tray.   This tray can be used in many different ways: as a bread basket, a letter tray, or as a holder for other objects. Detail 1 shows wires A and B being soldered in place for the basic frame. In detail 2, the grill wires (C) are soldered to the frame, and detail 3 shows wires D and E formed into the handle. (A clothespin and wooden block hold wires while they are being soldered.) In detail 4, the grill assembly is turned over and soldered to the handle. The result is a handsome, distinctive piece. Total cost: $1.

Table Tray

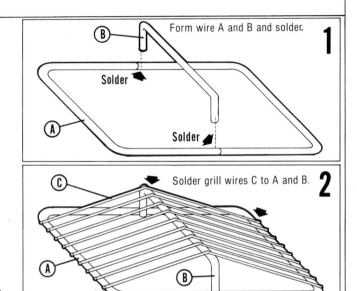

Form wire A and B and solder.

1

B

Solder

A

Solder

Solder grill wires C to A and B.

2

C

A

B

LETTER   DESCRIPTION

A   Square —12 gauge
B   Grill Support Wire —12 gauge
C   Grill Wires — 9; 16 gauge
D   Left Handle —12 gauge
E   Right Handle —12 gauge

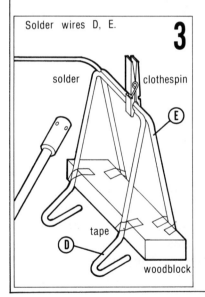

Solder wires D, E.

3

solder   clothespin

E

tape

D

woodblock

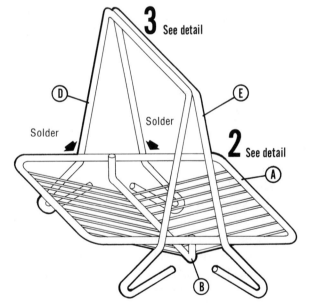

3 See detail

D

E

Solder   Solder

2 See detail

A

B

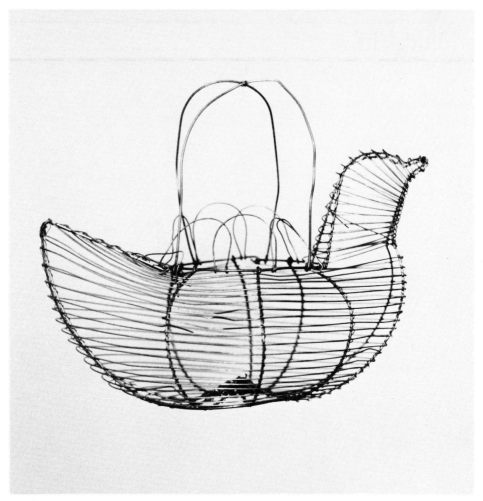

Bird Basket

Bird Basket.   (1) FRAME   To construct the frame, first make circle
A. Next cut two equal lengths of B wires and bend them to form the
tail. Crimp the ends of B around the rim of A as shown. Now cut two C
wires and bend them to shape the bird's head. Loop the ends of the
wires around circle A. Next cut six side wires (D) and bend and loop
them. Bring all the free ends of the D wires together on the bottom as
shown, and tie them securely with tie wire (see construction detail
plate for this procedure).

   (2) CONSTRUCTION DETAILS   Actually functioning as handles, the
"wings" (F) of the bird basket are shown in detail 1. Also, the overlap-
ping arches or U-shapes (E) form a movable "lid" for the basket, closing
shut when the handles are brought together. Loop these wires around
the circle A, as shown in detail 1. Detail 2 shows how the converging

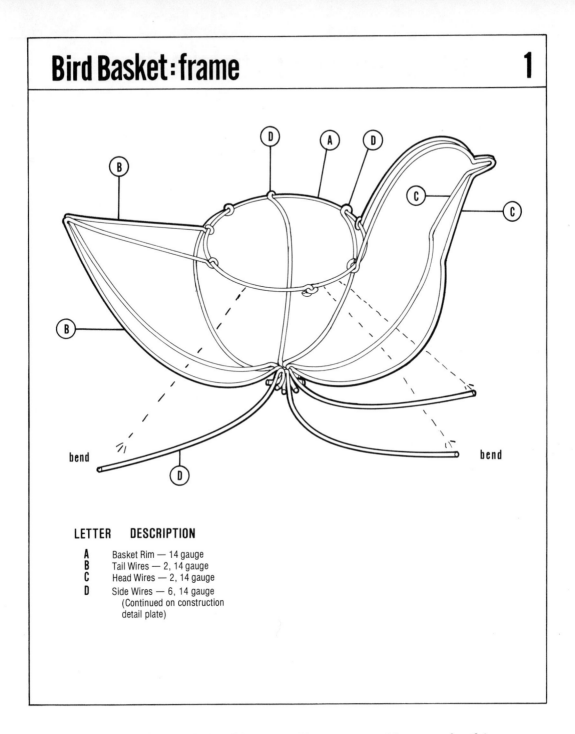

LETTER   DESCRIPTION

A   Basket Rim — 14 gauge
B   Tail Wires — 2, 14 gauge
C   Head Wires — 2, 14 gauge
D   Side Wires — 6, 14 gauge
        (Continued on construction
        detail plate)

ends of wires are tied with flexible wire. (You may try 22-gauge for this purpose.) The wrapping wire G is formed by coiling it around the basket frame. Secure the wrapping wire to the basket frame by neatly looping tie wires over and around as shown.

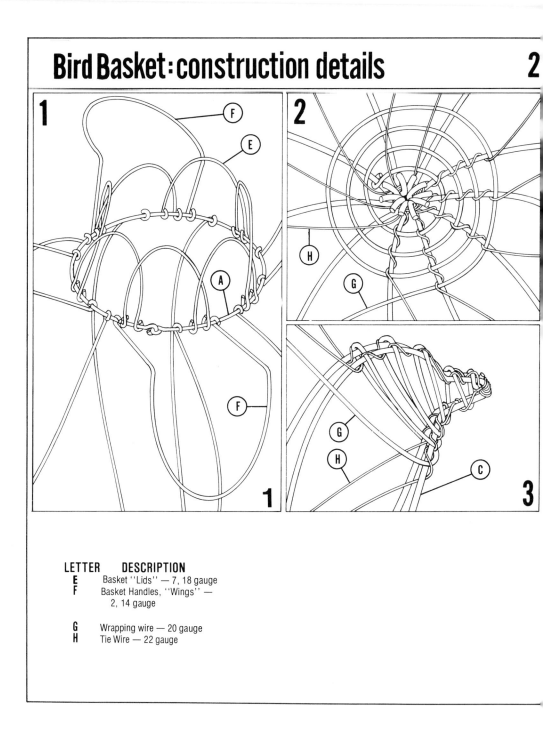

LETTER	DESCRIPTION
E	Basket "Lids" — 7, 18 gauge
F	Basket Handles, "Wings" — 2, 14 gauge
G	Wrapping wire — 20 gauge
H	Tie Wire — 22 gauge

Detail 3 indicates how the C wires forming the bird's head are connected. Notice that the tie wires are once again carefully looped over and around the G and C wires to secure the wrapping. Use this same procedure throughout the final construction of the basket.

Candelabra

These two table candelabra are distinctive pieces and very handsome in the home. One is small and simple and one large and ornate. The small piece, quite easy to make, requires only four wires bent according to design and soldered at specific points. The larger candelabra is highly decorative and quite a challenge.

Table Candelabra I.   A handsome table candelabra always comes in handy for decoration. This simple project uses four equal lengths of wire (D), as shown. Form these branch support wires carefully. Now cut a length of wire for the center post (A), and connect it to D wires by soldering. Attach the candle retainers (B) and the collars (C) to the ends of A and D. (Use ½-inch copper tubing for the candle retainers and five metal washers or lugs drilled with ⅛-inch holes for the collars.) The holes in the collars slip over one end of wire D and are epoxied into place; B is then glued to C.

Eight-gauge wire is very sturdy for this project, although 10g can be used. Paint or spray the candelabra black or gold.

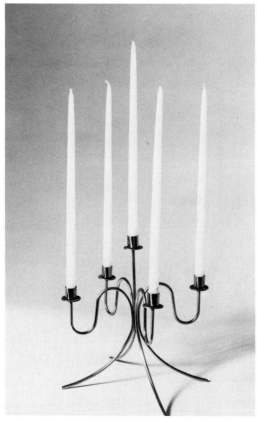

Table Candelabra I

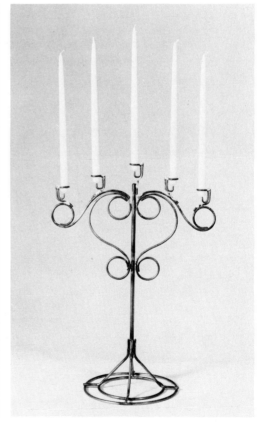

Candelabra II

83

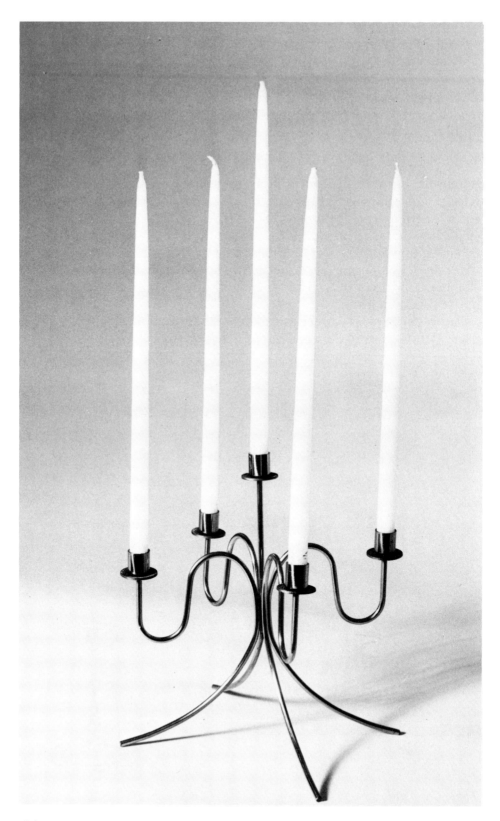

Table Candelabra 1

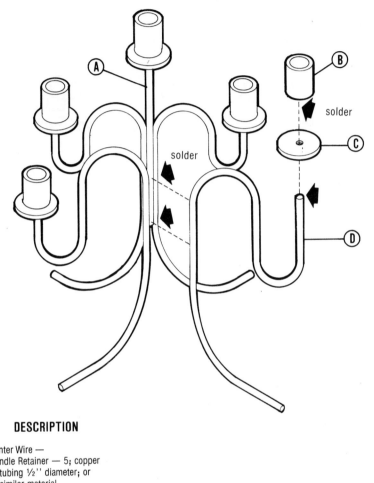

solder

solder

LETTER	DESCRIPTION
A	Center Wire —
B	Candle Retainer — 5; copper tubing ½'' diameter; or similar material
C	Candle Retainer Collar — 5; metal washers, or metal slugs (from knock-outs on electrical junction boxes); drill 1/8'' hole in center
D	Branch Support — 4

Candelabra II. This handsome candelabra takes some doing. Start with the basic center support rod (A); now cut and form the side arches (B) and solder at appropriate points. Shape and form the top arches (C) and solder in place. Make the platform next: this is an outer ring (E)

CANDELABRA 2 top construction

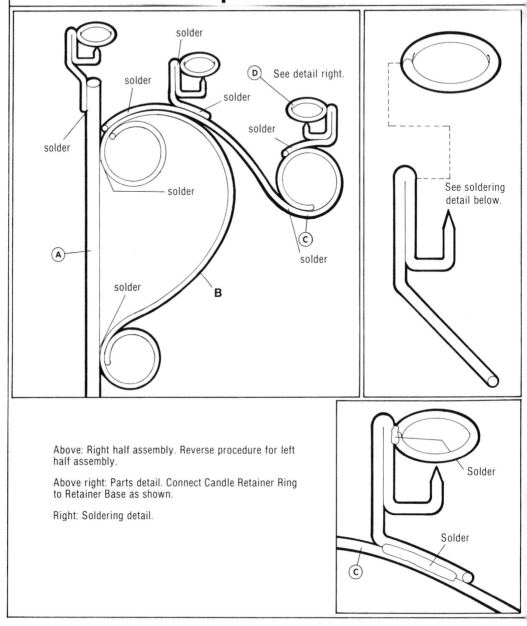

solder

solder

solder

D See detail right.

solder

solder

solder

solder

solder

A

solder

B

C

solder

See soldering detail below.

Above: Right half assembly. Reverse procedure for left half assembly.

Above right: Parts detail. Connect Candle Retainer Ring to Retainer Base as shown.

Right: Soldering detail.

Solder

Solder

C

and an inner ring (F); bend the support legs (G) and solder to the two circles and the support column (A). The candle retainer rings are small circles (D) and are soldered to the formed retainer bases (H) which are soldered to the top arches (C) and one unit to column A.

CANDELABRA 2 base construction

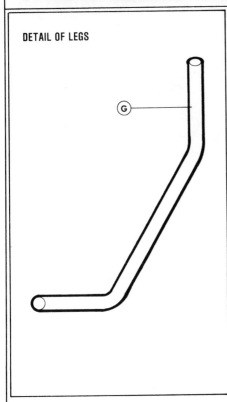

DETAIL OF LEGS

G

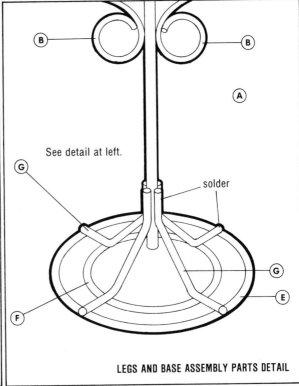

B

B

A

See detail at left.

G

solder

G

E

F

LEGS AND BASE ASSEMBLY PARTS DETAIL

Bend Center Support Bar Legs as shown. solder to
Center Support Bar and Base Rings as illustrated at right.

LETTER	DESCRIPTION
A	Center Support Bar — 8 gauge
B	Side Arches — 2; 10 gauge
C	Top Arches — 2; 10 gauge
D	Candle Retainer Rings — 6; 12 gauge
E	Base Outer Ring — 8 gauge
F	Base Inner Ring — 8 gauge
G	Center Support Bar Legs — 4; 8 gauge
H	Candle Retainer Bases — 6; 12 gauge

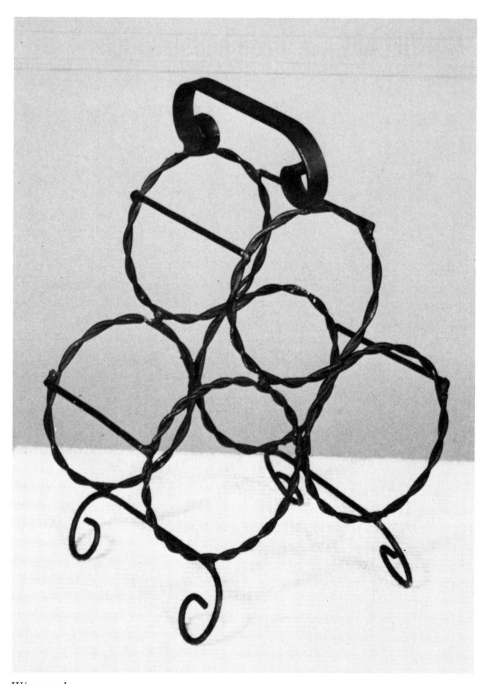

Wine rack

Wine Rack

If you are going to keep wine at home, you will need some type of rack to keep the bottles horizontal. This easy-to-make wire rack does a fine job; it is merely six twisted wire circles (B) (twist the wires as

Wine Rack

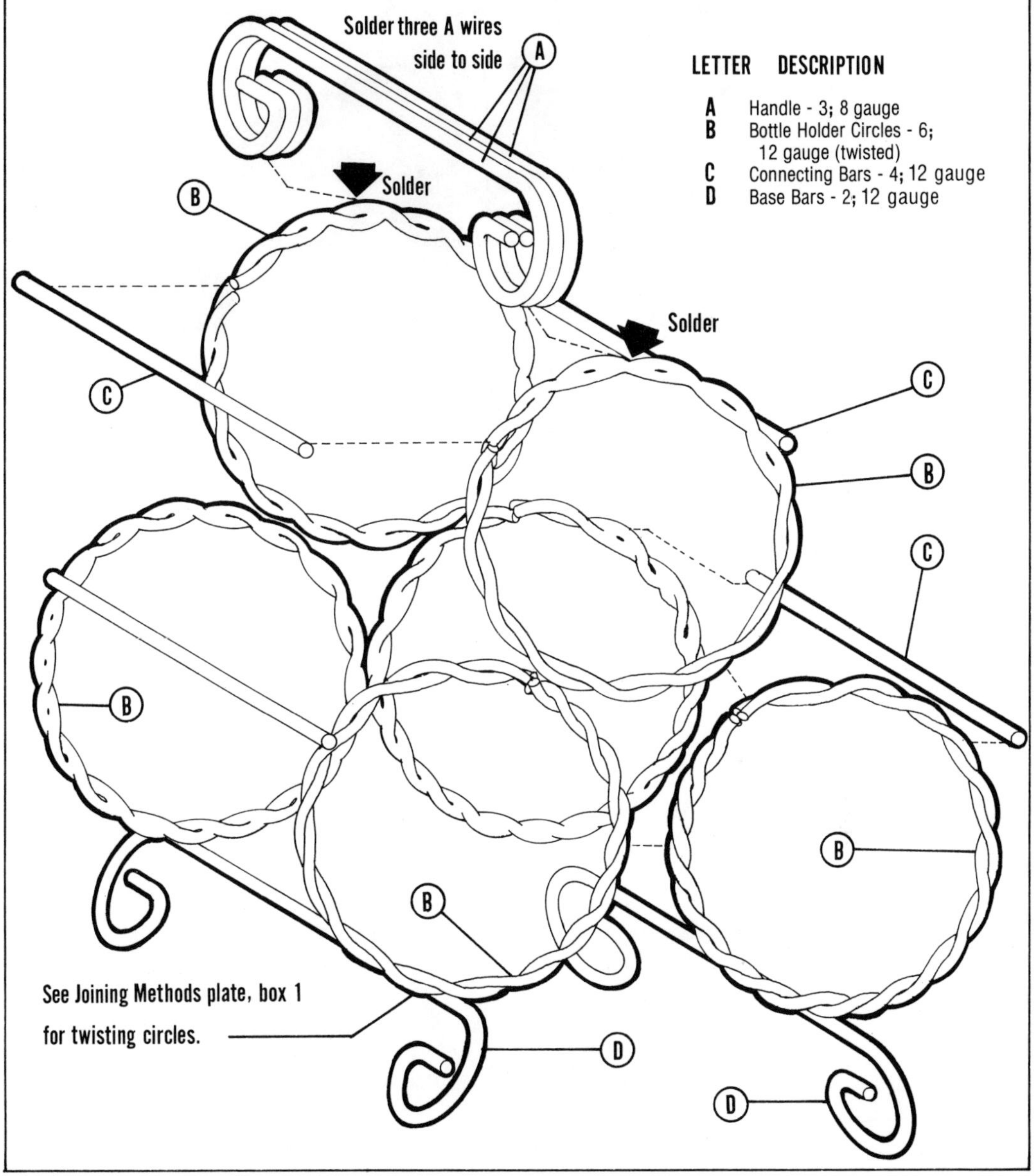

Solder three A wires side to side (A)

Solder

(B)

(C)

Solder

(C)

(B)

(C)

(B)

(B)

(B)

(B)

See Joining Methods plate, box 1 for twisting circles.

(D)

(D)

LETTER	DESCRIPTION
A	Handle - 3; 8 gauge
B	Bottle Holder Circles - 6; 12 gauge (twisted)
C	Connecting Bars - 4; 12 gauge
D	Base Bars - 2; 12 gauge

instructed in the plate-rack project). Solder connecting bars (C) to the circles at appropriate points, and solder the base bars (D) to the bottoms of the circles, as shown. Solder handle (A) (sheet metal) to the top of the B circles. If you do not have a piece of sheet metal, solder together three pieces of wire as shown in the drawing.

Wine rack

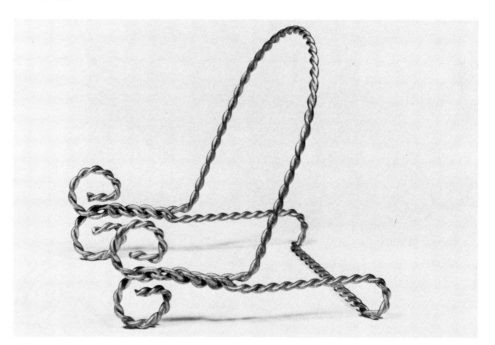

Plate rack

Plate Rack

This ornamental support for a plate or a picture is simple to make and useful. This is basically a two-piece wire structure, the base piece (B) attached to top piece (A). The most difficult part of the rack assem-

PLATE RACK

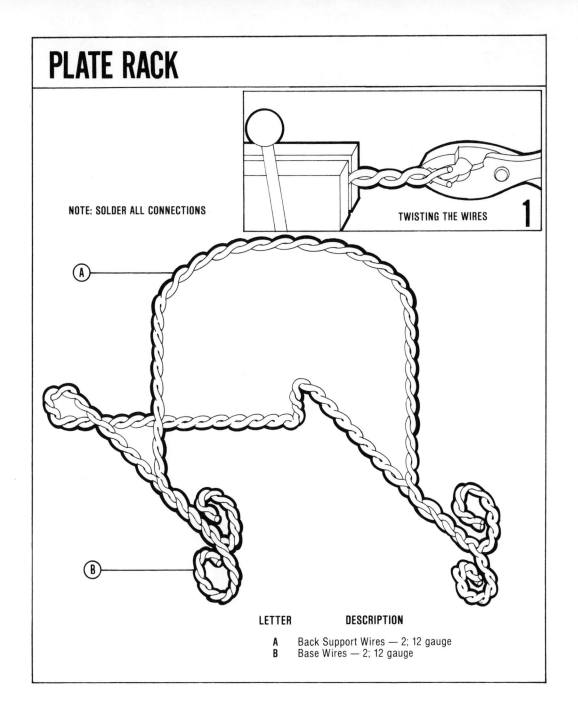

NOTE: SOLDER ALL CONNECTIONS

TWISTING THE WIRES **1**

LETTER	DESCRIPTION
A	Back Support Wires — 2; 12 gauge
B	Base Wires — 2; 12 gauge

bly is twisting the wire. To do this, clamp the base wire (B) securely in a vise as shown and bend.

We used 12g wire for this project, but 10g is also satisfactory, depending on the expected use of the item. For example, a picture requires a thinner wire than a very heavy plate. Spray the rack black or gold.

Plate rack

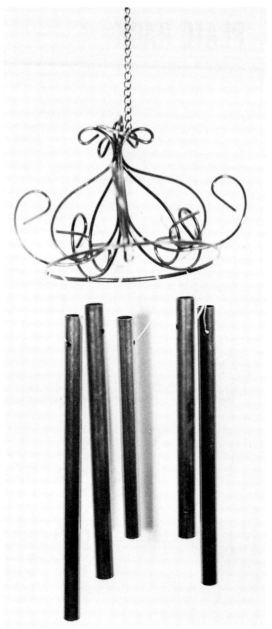

Wind chimes

Wind Chimes

Most of the pieces we have made from wire are used indoors, so here is one item for outdoors — a handsome, decorative wind chime. This piece is assembled in four steps. First, solder a 12-inch circle (A), as shown, or use a presoldered circle (sold at hardware stores). Bend the scroll work as shown for the top; this is a series of five S-curves (B), five crescent shapes (C), and a vertical wire (D) with eye hooks (E). Solder the pieces together (see detail 2), and solder them to circle A. The chimes (F) are metal or bamboo tubes with small ⅛-inch holes. Attach the tubes to C with fish line G (see detail 3). Next, attach chain I to the top of S-hook; attach I and H to E, as shown in detail 1. Use the wire as it is; no painting is necessary.

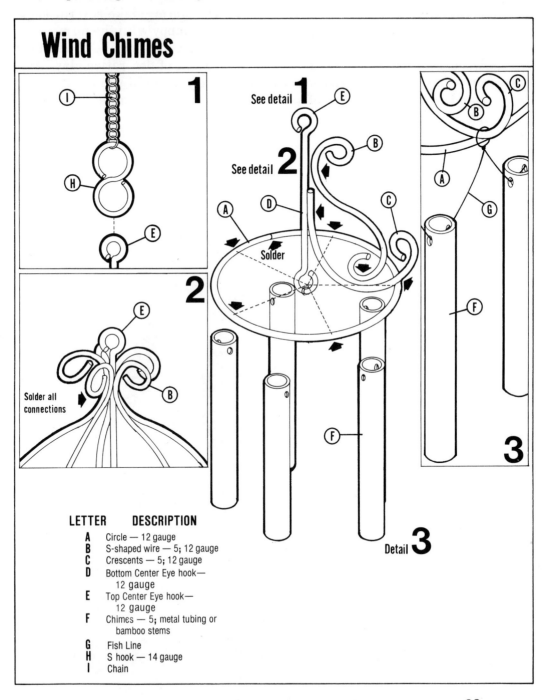

Wind Chimes

LETTER	DESCRIPTION
A	Circle — 12 gauge
B	S-shaped wire — 5; 12 gauge
C	Crescents — 5; 12 gauge
D	Bottom Center Eye hook— 12 gauge
E	Top Center Eye hook— 12 gauge
F	Chimes — 5; metal tubing or bamboo stems
G	Fish Line
H	S hook — 14 gauge
I	Chain

Human Form

This last project was done for fun and for decoration; it is a wire sculpture and so simple I felt it deserved inclusion in this book. This little figure can be placed on a table or desk for pure folly. First make the basic form from wire A. Then start wrapping wire B (see inset) and continue to wrap and loop around the basic form. Make several loops and keep accumulating layers until you are happy with the form.

If you have trouble keeping the figure erect it can be glued to a wooden block or simply embedded in a chunk of decorative clay. And once you have made this one wire sculpture you might want to try your hand at making others of your own choosing — an animal shape or perhaps even a mask.

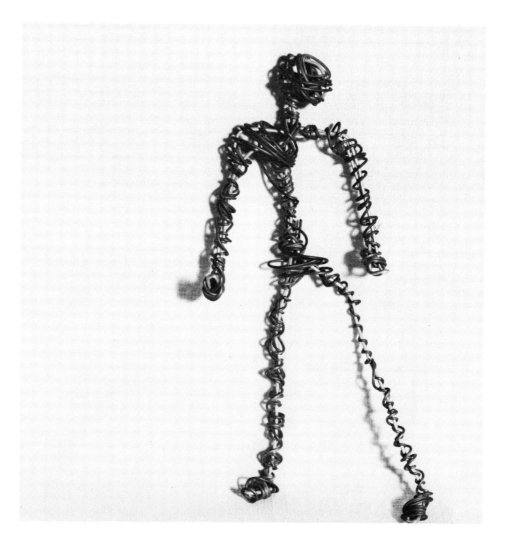

Human Form

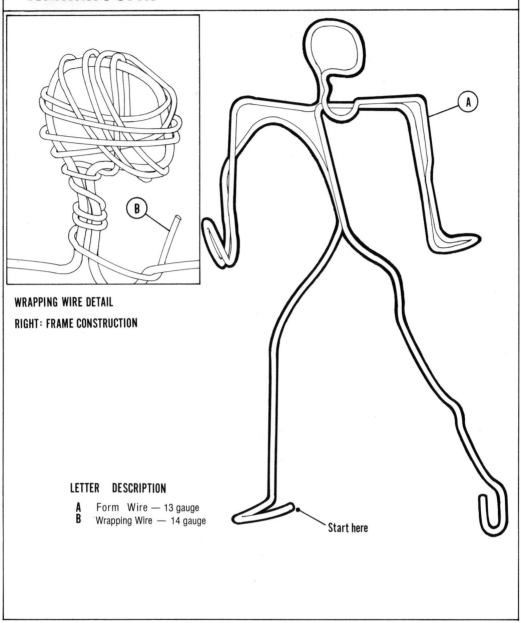

WRAPPING WIRE DETAIL

RIGHT: FRAME CONSTRUCTION

A

B

Start here

LETTER	DESCRIPTION
A	Form Wire — 13 gauge
B	Wrapping Wire — 14 gauge

8 Furniture

Tables, shelves, plant stands, and magazine racks can be made of wire — at practically no cost, compared with what you would have to pay for them if you bought them ready made.

End Table

This piece can also be used as a coffee table. The basic table frame (B) is made first; cut wire and solder to make a rectangle. Now bend

END TABLE

LETTER	DESCRIPTION
A	Top Grill Wires — As many as needed; 10 gauge
B	Table Frame — 8 gauge
C	Table Legs — 4; 8 gauge

NOTE: SOLDER ALL CONNECTIONS

and shape table legs (C) and solder at corners. The top grill wires (A) are soldered in place last; space them evenly. The table can hold books or any large flat object; set a glass pane on top to make it an all-round coffee table.

Easy to make and very handsome painted black. Total cost: $3.

Magazine Rack

A really useful item, a magazine rack is always needed to keep magazines in one place. This rack is simple to make, looks good, and costs little. First form two side wires (A). Now form two S-shaped wires (D), and solder them to sides A. Next, cut all support wires (B), space them as shown, and solder them in place on top of the A wires. Finally, solder

Magazine Rack

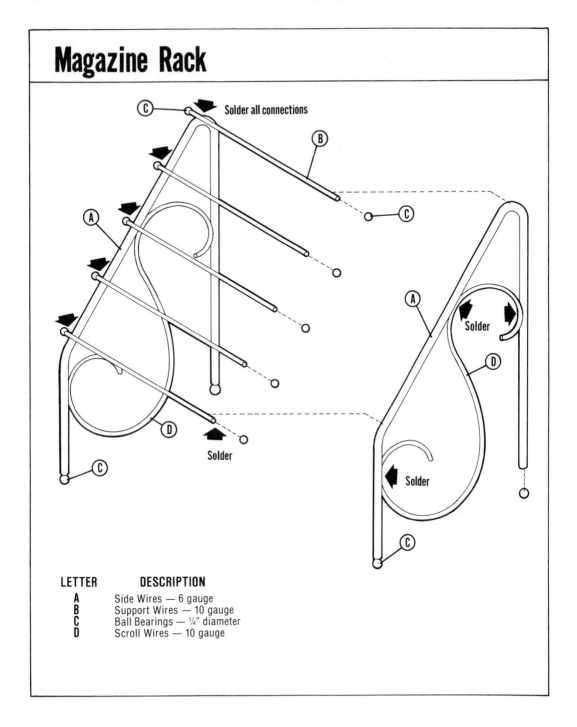

Solder all connections

Solder

Solder

Solder

Solder

LETTER	DESCRIPTION
A	Side Wires — 6 gauge
B	Support Wires — 10 gauge
C	Ball Bearings — ¼" diameter
D	Scroll Wires — 10 gauge

ball bearings (C) at ends of A and B wires to complete the utilitarian rack. (*Note*: ball bearings can be eliminated.)

The rack may be finished in black paint or any other suitable finish or left natural, coated with clear plastic.

99

Shelf Caddy

This useful shelf caddy uses looped wires (F) for ornamentation and wire screen or grillwork (E) for the shelves. Form the F loops. Next form the roof wires (B) and solder them at the top of circle A. Next,

Shelf caddy

Shelf Caddy

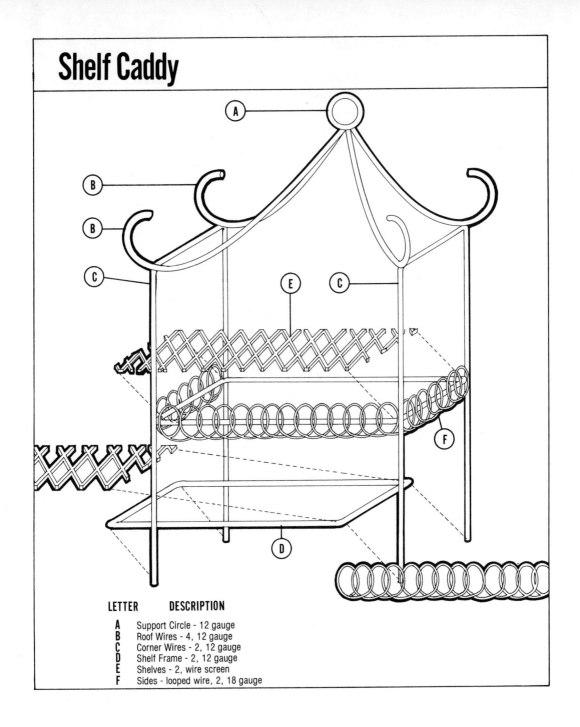

LETTER	DESCRIPTION
A	Support Circle - 12 gauge
B	Roof Wires - 4, 12 gauge
C	Corner Wires - 2, 12 gauge
D	Shelf Frame - 2, 12 gauge
E	Shelves - 2, wire screen
F	Sides - looped wire, 2, 18 gauge

solder the B wires at four points to corner wires (C), and solder shelf frames (D) to C wires. Glue the ornamentation wires to the outside of the D shelf frames. Finally, glue the shelves (E) to D. (*Note:* you can buy perforated grillwork at hardware stores.)

Tall Plant Stand

If you have houseplants, here is an attractive stand that will dramatically elevate and display your plants. The plant stand is constructed from four vertical wires (B), looped at the ends and curved as shown. Bend and form wires as indicated in the drawing. Wires A, D, and C form the fold-up brace (see detail 1); solder these wires to the B

Tall Plant Stand

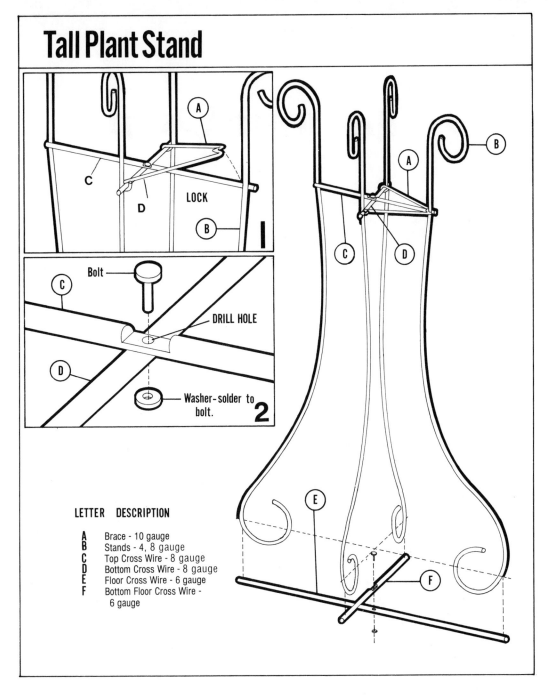

LOCK

Bolt

DRILL HOLE

Washer-solder to bolt. **2**

LETTER DESCRIPTION

A	Brace - 10 gauge
B	Stands - 4, 8 gauge
C	Top Cross Wire - 8 gauge
D	Bottom Cross Wire - 8 gauge
E	Floor Cross Wire - 6 gauge
F	Bottom Floor Cross Wire - 6 gauge

wires at joints. Use a bolt and washer at the intersection of the C and D wires, as shown in detail 2. At the base of the stand, solder wires E and F to the bottom of the four B wires.

The unit is handsome and functional and folds up when not in use. Set a potted plant in place at the top; the plant will be secured by the curves of the top wires. A totally unique way to display your plants.

9 On Your Own

Once you are hooked on wire, you'll want to go beyond the projects in this book. Why not decorate a box with filigreed wire? Or learn to do wire embroidering, a craft in itself, which produces handsome pictures? Or you might want to make wire silhouettes. Finally, if the art world is calling, you can try to create sculptures in the Calder tradition, where the wire is a totally expressive medium.

Decorating Boxes

Any wooden box or similar container works well for wire decorating. Select a pattern for the box; you want an overall design, so first make a sketch on paper so you'll have something to follow.

When the design has been created, shape wire by forging it to conform to the pattern. When the pieces for the total pattern are bent and hammered flat, mix the epoxy and thinly cover the surface of the box. Apply the epoxy resin to the surface with a spatula, and try to get an even coating (one of the 5-minute hardening epoxies will work best). Now, imbed the wire design into the epoxy. After the first layer hardens, apply another layer of epoxy. You can actually apply as many layers as you desire (after each layer dries). After you have built up the epoxy layers, sand the surface to eliminate any imperfections, and then apply a final layer of epoxy.

Filigree

The lacelike effect of filigree work is beautiful, especially when fine silver wire is used. When the wire is hammered, it can be easily shaped into intricate and small seashell or circle patterns.

Filigreed wire is formed with fine-pointed pliers and hand work; the designs are intentionally tight: All wires must touch so soldering can be done. In filigree work the outer structure is soldered first with heavier wire, and then the negative areas are filled in with silver swirls and

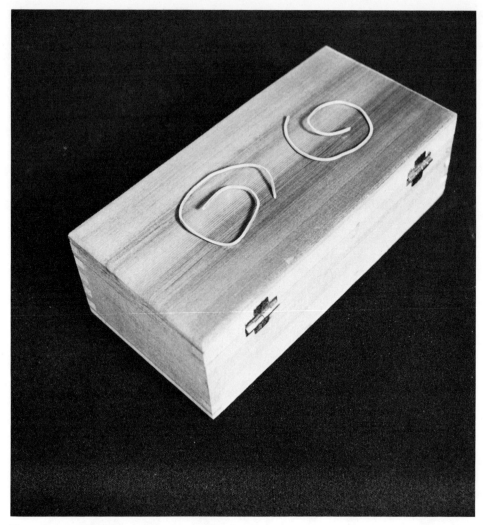

*Two decorative shapes of wire applied
to a wooden box with epoxy.*

coils. These shapes are fitted into the larger outer frame with tweezers and your fingers.

Filigree work is done with a solder flux powder. Mix the bits of solder with flux, 10:1, and then spread the mixture over the entire filigree. Using a propane torch, solder with a low flame, and after each soldering quench the piece in cold water.

Wire Embroidery

Embroidering wire through ordinary screen can produce lovely effects. Like the grid cloth used in needlepoint, the wire screen is a suitable background for wire embroidery work. The finished product can be a wall hanging, or it can be attached to any flat surface like a box or plaque. The skillful can achieve a startling, colorful tapestry by using thin strands of colored wire, such as copper or brass.

The space between the screening is just large enough for thin wires to pass through. Be patient; each wire has to be passed through the tiny grid openings. Secure strands with pliers, making tiny knots on the back of the screening. Experiment and see what you can do; this is yet another way of using versatile wire.

An example of filigree wirecraft.

Silhouettes

You have probably seen wrought-iron silhouette work in fences and gates. The same principle can be applied to wire sculpture in a one-dimensional process. First sketch the pattern on paper, using uncomplicated but effective scenes. Select different gauge wires for the scene, to create dimension.

For your silhouette, first make a suitable frame — rectangular, square, or circle. The beauty of the silhouette is in continuous lines soldered to the frame at several points. In some cases the wires can be attached with glue instead of solder. Solder or glue can also be used to hold wire together in the picture itself, but a better way is to use the continuous wire shape. Start with a small piece; eventually you will be able to create some beautiful effects. Forged as well as standard wires work well in this process.

Wire Art

Much fine wire art, such as Calder's works, is frequently exhibited in various art galleries. Indeed, wire has been used extensively in recent decades in wire sculptures, and the results have been very gratifying. Faces, figures, forms, mobiles, abstract standing wire works, and so forth have been done with exceptional beauty; and the more you work with wire, the more you will realize its tremendous versatility as both a useful material and a decorative one.

Designs are infinite, and what you make depends only on your own talents. If the household items we have suggested have intrigued you, you might want to further pursue wire as an art form. It is something you can do with your own hands and imagination, and it opens the door to a totally new, yet old, way of making things yourself.

10 Finishes

Wire can be used for many items as it comes from the roll or spool, but for a more finished look, wire must usually be painted or finished with a clear plastic coating to preserve the wire. Most household items like baskets and magazine racks can be painted black for a handsome effect — black is universally a good color for these functional items. White, gold, silver, and copper colors also lend themselves well to wire and are attractive finishes. Painting is necessary in wall sculptures and more decorative pieces, because the items are composed mostly of negative space, so the lines will show up sharply against any background only if they are painted. Always ask for paint for metal surfaces; there are many at suppliers.

Cleaning

No matter what kind of wire you are coating or what coating you are using, the wire must be absolutely clean or the finish will not adhere to it properly. Wire absorbs the oil from your hands and has its own inherent coating of oil, dust, and dirt that you may not see. Be sure to clean the wire thoroughly with soap and water, and then rinse and dry it thoroughly. But washing wire is not easy when the object is already assembled. Use a large sponge and soap and water, and then, if possible, take the piece outside and hose it down to rinse it off completely. Let it dry in the air, or use a dry cloth and wipe it dry.

Painting

There are three ways to apply paint to wire: (1) brushing, (2) spraying, and (3) dipping. Brushing is the most difficult because it is laborious, especially if the piece to be painted is large, like a mirror frame, for example. Brushing also requires two or three coats, can be messy, and is usually expensive because you have to use very fine artists' brushes.

If you do brush paint, apply a *thin* paint evenly and slowly. This is easier than it sounds: If the object is on a flat surface, the paint has a tendency to spread to the covering on the surface, and then the item must be turned over for painting on its reverse side. (Round items are even harder to paint.) Let the first side dry before you paint the reverse side.

If you decide to paint the wire item in a vertical position (and I tend to favor this process), buy a block of Styrofoam and plunge one end of the wire item into the block so you can have the item in front of you at eye level. In this way there is no turning and waiting for paint to dry; you can do one surface of the wire piece, swing the block around, and paint the other surfaces. However, the problem with vertical painting is that paint may flow downward, which can become messy. For vertical painting it is best to use a slightly thick paint.

Spray painting (with aerosol can paints) is quite fast and easy but expensive. The wire stand I made and painted white required three cans of paint. You may think one can will cover, but remember that wire is round and open, so all surfaces must be covered, unlike wood, which has only one flat surface. Buy enough paint because it is a bother to stop and run out for more once the project is under way.

To spray paint, select an outdoor area if at all possible (I do my painting under an open garage door). Set up a waist-high work table, and implant the piece into a Styrofoam block with a wire, so you can see the object from all angles. I tack a large cardboard against a wall about 5 feet from the object to be painted and aim the spray in that direction, so paint does not float to other areas. Use the standard spray paints.

When you use spray paint, keep the can about 6 to 7 inches from the object, and spray in a uniform rhythm, up and down, side to side, in one continuous application. Spot spraying results in buildup of paint in one area. Apply paint from both the top and bottom; hold the can at an angle for underneath and top painting. Try to cover all exposed areas, and keep moving. If you want to apply a second coat (and this is usually necessary), let the first coat dry thoroughly before applying the second coat. If it is a windy day, the paint will deposit itself on you no matter how careful you are.

Dipping is really the most professional way of painting your wire piece. It does involve some equipment, but it so easy and fast to dip pieces that it is worth the investment. Also, I think dipping gives a more even and attractive coating to wire than brushing or spraying. (And because of the uproar over aerosol sprays, dipping may be the safest and wisest choice.)

To dip a piece, you will need a watertight pan or tray as large as the object you want to paint. This might be impractical for, say, magazine racks and such, but for small nameplates and wall sculptures you can use bread-baking tins. Pour the paint into the tin to a depth of about 1 inch; then hold the wire item with tongs and set it into the paint for a few seconds. Remove the object and let it drain off excess paint. To dry the piece, set it horizontally on two bricks spaced a proper distance apart. Touchup can be done with a brush where the piece rests on the bricks.

If you do not have tongs, use any similar kitchen tool to hold the object. However, tongs (especially spaghetti tongs) are best; use two pairs so you can grasp the wirework at both ends and lower it into the paint tray in a level, horizontal position.

Plastic and Other Coverings

If the color of the wire is suitable for the object being made, protect the wire from moisture, rusting, or erosion by using a clear plastic finish. These are applied in the same way as spray paints.

Paint and clear plastics are the accepted methods of finishing wire, but you can do other things, too. Wrap strips of aluminum foil around wire to give the piece a silver finish. A very good method of decorating the wirepiece is to wrap ⅛-inch strips of colored quille paper (at arts and crafts stores) around the wire. Quille paper comes in coils, is inexpensive, available in many colors, and gives the wire item a festive character that is sometimes desirable. First, apply a light coating of glue to the wire, and then wind the paper in place to create a very handsome effect.

Another wire covering is Con-Tact paper; cut it into strips and, using its own adhesive-back, apply it to the wire as you would paper.